From Darkness to Light

Angela Rodgers

Be Blessed

BATTLE PRESS
SATELLITE BEACH, FLORIDA

From Darkness to Light

Copyright © 2022 by Angela Rodgers

All rights reserved. No part of this book may be used or reproduced by any means, graphic, electronic, or mechanical, including photocopying, recording, taping or by any information storage retrieval system without the written permission of the publisher or author except in the case of brief quotations embodied in critical articles and reviews.

From Darkness to Light may be ordered through booksellers or by contacting:

Angela Rodgers
www.Angelamrodgers.com
Contact@Angelamrodgers.com

Or

Battle Press
steve@battlepress.media
www.battlepress.media

ISBN: 979-8-9862-6320-5 (SC)
ISBN: 979-8-9862-6321-2 (eBook)
Library of Congress Control Number: 2022908839

Printed in the United States of America

First Edition

TABLE OF CONTENTS

DEDICATION 5
ABOUT THE AUTHOR 6
PREFACE 8
DISCLAIMER 9
CHAPTER ONE A NOTE FROM ANGELA 10
CHAPTER TWO MY GENESIS 13
CHAPTER THREE THE RODGERS EST. 1964 24
CHAPTER FOUR YOU ARE ONLY AS SICK AS YOUR SECRETS 32
CHAPTER FIVE DESTRUCTION OF LITTLE FAITH 45
CHAPTER SIX THE RINK 53
CHAPTER SEVEN MEETING NATAS 62
CHAPTER EIGHT DOWNSLIDE INTO WICCA 68
CHAPTER NINE WITCHCRAFT 101 72
CHAPTER TEN THE RECRUITMENT 78
CHAPTER ELEVEN THE BAD, WORSE AND UGLY 86
CHAPTER TWELVE QUESTIONABLE TRUTHS 93
CHAPTER THIRTEEN WICCA FAR AND WIDE 100
CHAPTER FOURTEEN HISTORY REPEATS ITSELF 110
CHAPTER FIFTEEN THE PARTIAL DEMISE OF TRINITY AND WICCA
.... 117
CHAPTER SIXTEEN THE EXTIRPATION UNFOLDING 121
CHAPTER SEVENTEEN THE AWAKENING OF FAITH 135
CHAPTER EIGHTEEN PAINFULLY BROKEN 144
CHAPTER NINETEEN MOTIVATIONS FOR SERVING GOD 152

- CHAPTER TWENTY BEAUTIFULLY REDEEMED 158
- CHAPTER TWENTY-ONE SERVANT HEART AND HANDS 165
- CHAPTER TWENTY-TWO IN THE LIGHT OF ETERNITY 170
- CHAPTER TWENTY-THREE CONCLUSION: GOD'S PRETTY SMART 176
- CHAPTER TWENTY-FOUR THE WHOLE ARMOR 182
- CHAPTER TWENTY-FIVE INVENTORY YOUR ARMOR OF GOD .186
- CHAPTER TWENTY-SIX THE TRUTH BEHIND THE CRAFT THE GOOD, BAD AND UGLY 189
- CHAPTER TWENTY-SEVEN WHAT AM I ABOUT TO WRITE?.......193
- CHAPTER TWENTY-EIGHT WHAT THE HELL DID I JUST READ?.201
- CHAPTER TWENTY-NINE A GLITCH IN REALITY..........................206
- CHAPTER THIRTY HOW TO MAKE HEAVEN YOUR HOME 210
- CONNECT WITH ME?...216

DEDICATION

Mom

I am who I am because of who you are. I would not be who I am today if you didn't put me on that bookshelf.

ABOUT THE AUTHOR

Angela M. Rodgers is unapologetically a lover and teacher of Christ. This relationship was fortified even greater as God restored her through the deaths of her two sons. She is a native of Michigan and enjoys her country living with her kids and husband, Myke. Angela and her husband have adult children, grandchildren, and dogs, but equally important, she has been the foster parent of more than 50+ children.

Even in all that, Angela is a preacher, Court Appointed Special Advocate (CASA) volunteer, and works to rescue women who have been victims of sex trafficking. Angela is a fierce advocate for children, and this type of advocacy is only birthed out of true adversity. She is not afraid to share the raw and personal details of her tragedies and grief to help others understand God's redeeming and healing love. Her testimony is her healing. Her testimony will be the catalyst to your healing as well.

As an average everyday woman and mother, Angela seeks to share her journey and redeeming love of God with you and others. She has a powerful story of resilience, faith, grief, and surrender delivered with humor and bluntness.

PREFACE

From Darkness to Light is a compelling story of the Author's journey of how she crawled out of the pits of the dark side of Wicca and Paganism to the light side of her faith in Christianity.

This is a true story of her walk through two decades of being a Wicca High Priestess. This voyage guided her to faith and led her to what she now believes is her Savior and Redemption with the Lord Jesus Christ.

It is a unique testimony with many losses and life lessons along the way.

It is the story of how God disciplined her when she hardened her heart and started rebelling and traveling the Wide path and not the Narrow road. Not many people can say that they received a 'Do-Over' like this.

This is a personal story, and any information contained herein is for the sole purpose of information. It is the writer's unique story. It is her family's personal story as seen thru her eyes.

DISCLAIMER

The Author tried to recreate events, locations, and conversations from her memories. To maintain their anonymity in MOST instances, she changed the names of individuals and places. She may have changed some identifying characteristics and details, such as physical properties, occupations, and areas of residence.

The content in the book all comes from the author's recollections, though they are not written to represent word-for-word transcripts. Instead, the author has retold them to evoke the feeling and meaning of what was said.

The publisher and the author are providing this book and its contents on an "as is" basis and make no representations or warranties of any kind with respect to this book or its contents.

CHAPTER ONE
A NOTE FROM ANGELA

This is written as a stand-alone nonfiction book; however, I previously wrote a book called *Painfully Broken Yet Beautifully Redeemed*.

When I wrote PBYBR, about the death of my two sons and my journey of Grief and Faith, I did not want my previous dark path of Wicca to overshadow my son's stories.

Understand it is complicated to write about religion in general. But writing about the journey that I had from Wicca to Christianity was challenging, healing, and in some cases, dangerous. It's hard sometimes to walk the path back down a broad road like this. Especially when opening the floodgates from hell again and putting it into print.

Some content is in both books to stay true to telling the whole story. Although the stories do go hand in hand, I wanted them to stand on their own. Thank you for your understanding and for offering me grace while reading.

It is necessary to also point out by way of caution; please read each page knowing it is written with compassion and pain from my heart, especially for those who feel they are still fighting their way through their own journey.

Every page is written with love from my own experience during my life and all the suffering I caused during my path of Wicca.

For me, getting answers and clarity was the way out. Perhaps that is not the same for everyone, but for those who are also built that way, I hope this is helpful for you.

Understand that nothing in this book is meant to be contentious or antagonistic. When one speaks about truth and the path in a world where moral relativity is the most chosen daily practice, it is almost impossible to do so and be understood as coming from love.

This one concern alone caused me to "think and pray about writing" but not write this for five years. I apologize ahead of time if anything I write is offensive to anyone. I felt that it was time for my story to be told, although writing it was difficult and stirred up deep-felt emotions.

I know that this story will not be for everyone. I also know that sometimes it is easier to become offended than to look at change.

It gives me comfort to hope that perhaps my experience can ease someone else's suffering and lighten their journey.

I want to be transparent, if you have purchased this book in hopes of learning 'Wicca,' 'The Craft,' 'Spell-Work,' 'Witchcraft,' or the 'Wiccan Rede,' please do yourself a favor and close the book and return it now.

You are not going to find that here. You will find a story of my devout and triumphant faith in Jesus Christ and how I am in absolute Awe that he spared me for a much bigger purpose. There is a lot of scripture written in this book, I felt the need to have equal parts of the horrible darkness and the light to counter act the witchy stuff.

I hope that reading this book won't change your opinion of me or my path. I am not who I once was. I am unapologetically a lover of Christ. It took me longer than it should have to get where I am, and God knows I have a long way to go, but I am a work in progress, and I'm thankful for the opportunity to grow each day. After all, it is all in God's timing, not mine.

Much love and be blessed as you walk this journey with me.

Angela

CHAPTER TWO
MY GENESIS

To understand my story, it is sometimes best to start from the beginning. There is a beginning, middle, and end with any great story. However, in stories like mine, there is a beginning, middle, end, and then a complete screw-up, a re-do and then yet another screw-up, and finally a do-over, which is my actual story. It wasn't always pretty or easy, but it is what has made me who I am today. Taking a walk down memory lane sometimes can be interesting.

On April 10th, 1927, my Grandmother May was born into severe poverty. She has a great story of survival from her younger years of poverty and her abusive alcoholic first husband. That story on its own deserves its very own book and title. I might choose to tackle that one later.

So, I will begin with when my grandmother met my grandfather, Robert, who in all legality was my step-grandfather. But given that I never met or had an interest in solidifying a relationship with my biological Grandfather, my grandfather's name, in all terms, is Robert Baggett, a man I grew up with, and looked up to incredibly when I was a child.

My grandfather was born in 1959, raised in Michigan, and was stationed in California as a Petty Officer in the United States Navy. My grandmother was employed as a Practical Nurse at a Senior Citizen facility. Her supervisor at the time was married to another Sailor and decided to introduce my grandparents. My grandfather got a package deal at a very young age. He became a father to my mother, Flora, who was around 13 at the time, and her brother, who was close to 15. My grandfather was only 27 years old when he took on the responsibility of two acting-out teenagers, and my grandmother, who struggled with mental health issues due to Bipolar Manic-Depressive Disorder.

He was a man of high honor and the utmost integrity. I can with one hundred percent certainty say that he made sure his new family never wanted or needed anything. He was, and still is, one of the hardest-working men I know.

I remember stories my mother told me that broke my heart; about their years growing up when my grandmother was a single mother raising two children on her own. They were so poor, sometimes only able to have macaroni noodles and powdered milk for meals.

My mother would have to put cardboard in the bottom of her shoes to keep from walking on the ground beneath her. My favorite story was that she used beets for blush and lipstick because they couldn't afford traditional make-up.

My mother was most definitely a Navy brat, growing up in California, then getting to travel to Yokosuka, Japan, when my grandfather was stationed there. So, given the history, I know for certain that my grandfather was most definitely a huge blessing in my family's life. I highly doubt they ever ate macaroni and powdered milk again, and my mother likely had a new pair of shoes when needed, along with her first makeup set.

One story I remember that was so indicative of my grandfather's character was when I was about ten years old. Early one morning my grandfather and I were in the kitchen making ourselves breakfast. I remember this day because he and I were going to be going on a long trail ride on the horses. He was making toast in their nice four-slice stainless steel toaster. It was always covered with a handmade cover that my grandmother had made. Back then, this was popular. It was like a little hat for their toaster.

My grandfather pushed the lever that lowered the bread to begin toasting two times. He liked his toast burnt; he purposely ran his toast through the toaster twice to achieve the level of dark he wanted. I asked, "Grandpa, why don't you just turn the dial to make toast darker instead of toasting it twice?"

He replied, "Angela, I don't want your grandmother to burn her toast accidentally if I forget to set the dial back." I don't know why but this always stayed with me. He would take more time doing something instead of the easier way of doing it just in case he might forget to reset it so that my grandmother would not burn her toast.

Today I do the same thing; I like my toast, bagel, or English muffin a little crispy. I prefer it with just a little bit of darkness on it. I think about my grandfather each time I toast my bread or bagel twice because I don't want to cause my husband or children to burn theirs if I forget to reset the dial back myself.

I know to many this seems petty, but it has stuck with me for many years. It showed putting others above yourself and his empathy for my grandma.

Charles, my father, was born on April 9th, 1943, and raised in Indiana. He was the son of Charles and Dorothy Rodgers, had a sister named Marsha and a brother named Richard. My grandfather Charles was in the Army and was a veteran of the

Battle of the Bulge with Honors.

Growing up, I have great memories of visiting the lake house in Indiana. We would have yearly family reunions where we went down and stayed the night. I enjoyed spending time with my cousins Jeremy, Alerie, Troy, Niki, Traci, and the rest of the family.

We often slept in the screen room outside of the main house. We swam in the lake and swung from a rope hanging from a tree, having a contest on who could flip or dive the best off the rope into the water. Many times, we would sneak on the roof of the house and jump, swinging and landing in the lake. They had a handmade, wooden outhouse and changing room on their property, because my grandmother would chase us out of the house with a cooking spatula if we came into the house when we were wet. My grandmother was rough around the edges, never holding anything back. One day, my cousin Jeremy and I walked in the front door, and she chased us right out the back because we were in our swimming suits.

I remember as a child sleeping in the screen room outside with my brothers and cousins, and my Uncle Rick would walk around at night, scaring us. We always knew it was him, but we wouldn't leave the screen room in fear of the monster in the lake that he would tell us about. I can still hear my Aunt Melody yelling at him "Rick stop, that's enough."

One of my best memories is of my Uncle Boyd, who is married to my Aunt Marsha and the father of Niki, Jeremy, and Traci. Uncle Boyd was my favorite Uncle growing up. He taught me how to water ski at the age of about 7. I remember being in my little red skis with the black boot and placing them between his big skis. He then used his body to help boost me up into the water upright. Then when he thought I was ready he would let go of the rope, and my father would take me around the lake. He would take me on jeep rides and was just all-around fun, especially when he would tease the kids about removing his glass eye.

Living as far away as we did, we didn't get to see them all that much. But when we did, there was always many laughs and conversations. I especially remember hearing stories about my father when he was younger.

I have been told that he had a lot of spirit growing up. Some good and some perhaps not so good. Some family members have said my grandmother was extremely hard on him and sometimes unfair. I was told it might have been considered abusive in today's world. Others have said that he was just a defiant child and may have gotten what he deserved.

Given what I remember about my grandmother, and knowing my father, I can see where both could have come into play. But this is something I will never know. Each person has their version of the environment growing up.

I remember that my grandmother was very outspoken and never held anything back; she did lack a verbal filter. If you were wearing a bathing suit she didn't like, she would tell you it was ugly and looked terrible on you. I am very much outspoken, like my grandmother in many ways. The older I get, the more tactful I become. My grandfather was a tiny man, and I don't think I ever saw him upset or raise his voice. He was mild-mannered. He liked to tinker in his woodshop quite a bit. He built my first baby crib when I was born. It was small and rocked back in forth. I still have it today, and my niece used it as a baby and my children did as well.

From my understanding now, my father had gotten into some trouble, and he was given a choice at a court hearing to enter the Military or face the consequences. Different family members have other recollections of this. I am going by what my mother has told me.

He chose to go into the Marines (Oorah!) on May 18th, 1960, at the age of 17. My father was a Military Policeman (MP). Ironically enough, he entered the military with the same rank he left with. I suspect that he still maintained some of the childhood spirits I wrote about earlier.

He was stationed in Yokosuka, Japan. I have a few pictures of him on my refrigerator with young children he was helping during this time. So, Japan is where my story begins.

My parents met in December 1963 and dated for a total of seven months. Two of these seven months they spent apart due to my father coming back to the states for discharge of his tour of duty from the Marines.

Hearing stories about how my parents met, I now realize my mother had some childhood spirit to her as well. When she was about 17, she went clubbing off base one night with a group of friends. While waiting at a bus stop on base she was introduced to my father. According to my mother, he was a bit under the weather. Not under the weather as in the flu, common cold, or allergies. I understand now what "under the weather" meant from my childhood.

They got engaged on April 10th, 1964, and then my father left for the states the week after, leaving my mother behind to graduate high school on May 22nd, 1964, from Nile C. Kinnick High School in Yokohama, Japan. I have been told that the school is named after a Military Officer who resided in Iowa.

They married on July 3rd, 1964. It was always a joke of my father's while I was growing up that he lost his independence on July 3rd, to gain it back the following day, July 4th, on Independence Day.

They were married in my father's local church called Ormas Baptist Church in Columbia City, Indiana, with my Uncle Rick as a groomsman for my father, and my Aunt Marsha standing as a bridesmaid for my mother. My Mom was a beautiful bride, wearing a knee-length white dress with lace. She wore her hair smoothed straight with the bottom winged out, which was the style in those days, along with her pointed vintage eyeglasses. My father was her own Wally Cleaver from the show *Leave it to Beaver*.

At seventeen, my mother graduated high school, met my father, and got married before she turned 18. She picked up and moved across the country by herself, without any of her family, and married my father without looking back.

They started without a pot to pee in; they had

nothing but each other. After they were married, they lived for two months in a tiny apartment in Ligonier, Indiana. As my father worked in a local factory, they were barely making ends meet. They couldn't even afford a vehicle to get around in. They took the bus everywhere they needed to go.

My Grandfather's brother Wilber knew the struggle they were having and got my father a job with Ford Motor Company in Michigan. This was an answer to their prayers, so they wasted no time moving.

My parents packed their belongings and bought a one-way ticket on a greyhound bus. They made their way to Michigan, where my father began working at Ford Motor Company in Ypsilanti, Michigan. My father ultimately retired from Ford when I was a young adult.

This plan was well thought out, and it was always my grandfather's intention to return to Michigan with my Grandmother May after his discharge from the Navy. All his family lived here, including his parents, brother, aunts, uncles, and cousins. It seemed natural for Michigan to become our new home.

It is ironic how this all played out for my parents. I have heard it even called fate. My mother left all she knew and married my father in the town where he was born and raised. With none of her family living there, she still ended up in the state where her mother landed.

CHAPTER THREE
THE RODGERS EST. 1964

It was a boat of a car, a large black and white 1952 Mercury Monterey. My parents saved to purchase it at the cost of $450. Today the car would go for nearly $25,000 and is considered a classic. With just over 25,000 cars in production, they had no idea what they had purchased.

After speaking with my mother about this, I had to chuckle because I could just see the image in my mind. My mom sitting in the passenger seat of the car with her light brown hair that is flipped out on the bottom tips, sporting her vintage retro eyeglasses with my father driving the car as he always did; one hand on the top of the steering wheel with his thick black locks combed over to the side like always. Like I stated before, her very own Wally Cleaver.

These images comfort me to this day when I think of my parents. Just understanding their beginning helps me understand "our" beginning.

Our family began to multiply by three - the first arrival a bouncing baby boy named Robert Charles, who was born in October of 1965. Robert was always an intelligent child, well beyond his years. He was named after my grandfather and my father - two of the most influential men in my life.

Second coming in was my brother Kevin Wayne, born in September of 1968. He quickly got the nickname 'Bam Bam' because he was solid and had a temper to go with it. I remember times as a child when he would attempt to pick up a television and try to throw it at you if he was upset.

With the birth of Kevin, my parents decided to sell the four-bedroom home they had purchased on a land contract in 1965, located on Grand Blvd, in Ypsilanti, Michigan. Given my father's love of fishing, they agreed to buy a small two-bedroom home on a lake in Pinckney, Michigan.

Luckily it had a carport they converted into a third bedroom when they became pregnant with me in August of 1972, while they were in Ohio at Sea-World with my brothers.

I was literally "made in Ohio." I am a die-hard Michigan State fan; I bleed Green and White, so you know how this haunts me.

Last, but most certainly not least, my father got his baby girl. It had been decided that her name would be Dawn if they had a daughter. I know my mother had a different opinion and ultimately got her way. Angela Marie was born in May of 1973, entering the world completely bald and with the head shape of an onion. So, I got the worst from both ends. I was made in Ohio and looked like an onion.

My father called me "Ding" for no rhyme or reason from the moment I was born. There have been many jokes about this, but I was known as "Ding." I was a daddy's girl who could do no wrong in his eyes in many ways. I promise I did wrong, but I had my father wrapped around my finger as a young child. I'm sure my brothers would say that even as an adult, I did as well.

We grew up with thick burnt orange shag carpet on our floors and a big box TV. You know the ones with the 8-track tape and record player in the top of the cabinet. Our water was rust-ridden because we lived on the lake. I was sometimes embarrassed to have friends shower at our house because sometimes water came out of the pipes a copper color. It was a great luxury when we finally could afford a water softener to remove the rust from the water.

I have fond memories of spending Saturdays at the laundromat with my mom. Mom and I would wake up and go to the laundromat where I was able to play a few video games. Donkey Kong was my favorite, and Pac-Man was, and still is, my mother's. Often, we would eat lunch together.

We would sometimes run to the local K-Mart Café located in Brighton, Michigan, in the mall. I loved their submarines as a child. They had salami, bologna, honey ham, American cheese, super-thin sliced onions, sliced tomato, shredded lettuce, mustard, mayonnaise banana peppers, and the best pickle slices ever. I always ordered mine without the peppers or tomato. Add a frozen coke to the order, and for $3.00, you had a meal. My mom would grab a few and take them home to my brothers and father also.

We, as a family, did not have the most expensive or best of things, but we had everything we needed growing up.

Funny, or ok, not so funny story about my mother, God bless her soul. We just had new beige carpet installed in our living room, no doubt after a considerable amount of planning by my mom and dad. I was a speed skater at a local Roller Rink, and my skates were Jet-black with bright orange wheels, complete with black trucks and neon bright pink laces. I decided that I wanted to spray paint the skates pink to match the laces. This sounds like a great idea so far, doesn't it? So, I went to the shed, got a box, broke it down, and laid it flat on the carpet. I laid the skates on the box and spray painted them pink, but I did not account for the "overspray." My dear mother now had pink tinted carpet right in front of our big brown box Television. I am honestly surprised that I did not get sent to "boot camp."

My mother was just the type of person who offered so much grace, even when it was not deserved. I am not saying she was not mad. I remember her standing in the kitchen at the Island the next day; I saw her do this as I watched an episode of *The Dukes of Hazard* while sitting in the Living room. Just speaking of this, I am getting the butterfly feeling in my stomach and think to myself, "O crap, I'm in so much trouble." I remember looking up and seeing Mom tilt her head to the right with one hand on her hip and saying, "Is my carpet pink? Why is my carpet pink, Angela Marie?" "Ummm, yeah about that mom, I'm sorry."

My parents did the best they could, we didn't have the best of everything, but we most certainly had everything we needed. This doesn't mean that we didn't have our share of challenges.

It wasn't always "Rainbow and Unicorns." Sometimes that made things a bit rough, but from the outside looking in I am not specifically sure what others thought. As with any family with any dysfunction, ours was no different.

But there was always something missing in our home. Although it was not an intentional "Neglect," it shaped our home environment in a way that would have been different if we had just been raised in a home of Faith.

Even the best love stories have their own chapters of difficulty. It's not about just surviving the problematic moments; it is about healthily surpassing them. In difficult times we have a choice in how we respond to them. I'm not going to sit here and say that while I was growing up my family always responded appropriately to the many things that plagued our home. But I am one hundred percent sure of this: "My parents loved each other with everything they had through every chapter of difficulty." They loved each other through everything that came up in our home. For this, I am eternally grateful.

I will get very candid in the next chapter about some complicated topics including:

~Addiction

~Abuse and fighting, It's not always physical!

~Family roles in a dysfunctional home.

~Rehabilitation and how we as a family surpassed a statistic that blights our nation today.

There may be some triggers for readers in this chapter. So, I feel compelled to alert you to that fact. But I do feel like it is a story that needs to be told to help readers understand what your family foundation breeds is what your family foundation is. It is a cycle that will repeat itself repeatedly until someone breaks that cycle.

What do I mean when I say that there is a simple way to look at things?

~Trauma breeds traumatic life.

~Addiction breeds addiction.

~Abuse breeds abuse.

~Dysfunction breeds dysfunction.

But with this being said,

~Calm breeds Calmness.

~Rehabilitation breeds Restoration.

~Faith breeds Faithfulness.

YOU CAN AND WILL RECOVER from your hurt habits and hang-ups from your childhood. It will help if you chose to actively break the cycle of trauma, addiction, abuse, and dysfunction.

If you don't tend to the dysfunctional patterns

you've inherited from your family, you'll likely repeat them yourself. So, break the cycle before it can continue any longer. Start by giving leadership of every part of your life to God.

Commit yourself to do whatever God asks you to do during the change process. Stop the cycle of generational dysfunction. Yield your own will to God's will for you, trusting God to lead you to what's best when you face daily decisions.

CHAPTER FOUR
YOU ARE ONLY AS SICK AS YOUR SECRETS

Growing up in the Rodgers household was never dull. At times, one could even say it needed to be a bit more monotonous for our well-being. Especially in my younger years.

Previously I described the first meeting of my father and mother at the bus station. I had stated that he was under the weather. That was an excellent way of saying my father was intoxicated. My father was an alcoholic, a very functioning alcoholic at that. He never missed a day of work, never missed bringing an entire paycheck home, and was always there to tuck me into bed if he wasn't working. He was a great provider for our family. But at the end of the day, he was still an alcoholic.

When thinking about an alcoholic, many people have this image in their head that they are not able to function in society; this is the case for some but not for all. I was blessed that my father was functioning in his active addiction.

I can only remember a few times seeing him

intoxicated growing up. They are still very vivid memories of my childhood. I am sure there were many other times my mother or brothers would likely recall more. But I really can't. Looking back, I know why I can't remember more. I discuss the feeling of being the book on a shelf growing up in our household.

Once when I was younger, I was ice fishing with my Dad down the road on the canal we lived on. As we walked back down the street towards home, he was all wobbly and unable to walk straight. I can still feel the pressure on me as a child of age 5 or 6 to make sure he made it home safely that night.

I remember thinking to myself, "Daddy, please don't fall. I want to go play with my barbie house." I had just gotten it for Christmas, and it was my new favorite thing. This was the latest barbie dollhouse, having an elevator in it that went from the bottom to the top and a garage to park Barbie's pink corvette. It was the newest "in" thing that most little girls asked for. It was the only thing I had asked for Christmas that year.

I remember him leaning into me as we made our way down our road. As we walked into the front door of our house, he walked with me to my bedroom. He helped me get into my pajamas, and as he was leaning down, I could smell a strong peppermint odor coming from his mouth. As he straitened back up and began to tuck me into my bed, he fell backward into my brand-new Barbie dollhouse. He crashed through it, and it was now in pieces. My new favorite thing was now broken, and I couldn't understand what was wrong with my father. I thought he might be sick, not in an alcoholic way, but in the flu or worse way.

Looking back at my young childhood self from my now adult self, I remember thinking he had just been eating candy that he wasn't sharing because I could smell the peppermint from his breath. I know now that smell came from the peppermint schnapps he had been drinking. I just thought that he was sick, and that was why he fell into my dollhouse. At the age of 5 or 6, I made excuses for my dysfunctional family.

I remember a couple of other instances of my mother being upset with him for taking me to certain places he used to go to. I can honestly say with all certainty that even given what was taking place, my mother attempted to protect me from the dysfunction that surrounded us. I recently learned that my mother gave my father the ultimate ultimatum.

Little did we know it had just begun; my brothers

had witnessed much more than me. This, in essence, caused them both to start to develop their own addictive tendencies, including drugs and alcohol. Our family was spiraling out of control like a rollercoaster that was having a malfunction and stuck on "go".

This rollercoaster continued until 1981 when I was seven years old and mysteriously sent to stay a couple of weeks with my Aunt Oma and Uncle Arnold in San Diego, California. I had thought that I was just going on a vacation as I boarded a plane in Detroit, Michigan alone and flew to another state. Even while I was there, I was never told what was happening back home.

My mother gave my father the ultimate ultimatum, get help, or she was leaving. Not only did she threaten to leave my father, she also threatened to leave him with my brothers and take me with her. My brothers at that time were also causing havoc in the home with their addictions and behaviors as well. Like I said before, their love story was full of ups and downs, but they always were together.

My father went to a 14-day treatment program in Howell, Michigan, in April of 1981. He never touched another drink of alcohol from that day on. But the rollercoaster was not over yet; it was just beginning. In all honesty, things got way worse.

We had a family dog named Cory; it was a miniature curly gray-haired little poodle. It was also a drug-sniffing snitch of a dog. My brothers could never get away with hiding their drugs in our home because of the dog. Cory would just sit in front of wherever it was and bark uncontrollably until it was found. Mysteriously something happened to this dog. To this day, my mother and I have no clue. It just disappeared one day. Over the years, I have asked and have never been told. I most definitely have my suspicions about what took place, but I don't think we will ever know. I have repeatedly asked my brothers what they did to the dog, with no answer.

My parents quickly realized that one, our family dog was missing, and two, both of their sons were in active addiction as well. Sadly, my father getting sober did not automatically make my brothers follow suit. In fact, in many ways, it made family life harder.

My father was newly sober and trying to help my mother fix the mistakes that were made. This caused my brother's and my father to fight a lot. Often, they even got physical with fist fights. I remember one occasion that my mother left with me, and I came back home to my father with a broken leg. They had gotten into it and my father tripped on the step breaking his leg. The healthier my father became, the unhealthier my family looked because they were trying to gain control over the loss of power during my father's active addiction.

Robert ended up spending a week in lockup in Flint in 1981. He was busted selling to an undercover cop. Then to Fairview Deaconess in St. Paul, Minnesota, for treatment for 45 days. I also got the opportunity to visit this facility because it was a mandated family week for treatment before they allowed him to return home. He then went into treatment again in 1983 to Sacred Heart in Memphis, Michigan.

Kevin didn't shy away from trouble either. In 1981 he spent time in Toledo Hospital in Ohio. In 1982 he entered a 45-day program at Fairview Deaconess in St. Paul, Minnesota. I was excited to spend time again in Minnesota, even under the circumstances. Then in 1983, he spent some time in Eagle Village, in Hershey, Michigan. I learned recently that my parents temporarily put him in a foster home to get some further intervention for him and our family.

As for me, there was always so much going on in

the house. It felt like I was a novelty book most often, left on a shelf collecting dust. I was only brought out and dusted off to be shown to others. Every ounce of energy my parents had was spent helping my brothers or digging the house out of chaos. There was very little left for me at the end of the day.

Looking back now, I believe my mother did this to protect me from what was happening. I still witnessed some of it, but I was shielded from a lot of it for the most part. Even with all of this, I can still say that I had a great childhood. I indeed had my share of troubles, but I never got involved with drugs or alcohol; I was generally the designated driver in our group.

I did have a couple of mishaps with the law; when I was about 14. This happened at Meijer's, when my friend and I were walking around the store. We decided to steal an eyeliner. We quickly noticed a man following us around. We went to my mother, who was grocery shopping on the other side of the store at the time. My friend and I giggled and explained to my mom that a guy was flirting with us. It was gratifying for girls of our age having a grown man flatter us. So, we thought. Much to our surprise, this man followed us right out of Meijer's, stopping us and revealed his title as Loss Prevention. My mother hauled us right back into the store and into the loss prevention office. She was demanding that the police be called on us. Thanks to my brothers she had quite a few connections with probation officers and law enforcement in our hometown. This was of no help to myself or my friend in this situation.

Another time when I was younger. I was out with a friend and decided it would be a great night to test my mother's connections with law enforcement in our community. I am not sure why I decided to do this, as she was generally a step ahead of me. Most times, she knew before us kids even got home what we did, with whom we did it, and what trouble it caused. My brothers paved the way for her to know every law enforcement officer in our area.

I decided anyway to test the theory and stay out all night. Mom was able to track me down, telling the police officer that they better beat my father to where I was at, or it may be a different type of 911 call coming in. My father was a tiny man, but he knew how to handle himself if needed, especially when it had to do with me. My two older brothers were always willing to if he did not handle it. I will tell you I was more worried about my father getting a hold of who I was with, not the police. After being punished, I never stayed out all night again.

Looking back at my family, I honestly don't know how my mother survived everything. It seemed like a never-ending cycle for years. We had the family roles of a dysfunctional family. I believe we had them all covered.

~The Addict, Check.

~The Hero, Check.

~The Enabler, Check.

~The Scapegoat, Check.

~The Mascot, Check.

Recovery happened in our family but it took some time for everything to align as it should have. We were known as the "poster family" for dysfunction and rehabilitation. As a family, we often did open talks and training for other families going through the same thing as us. As a child, I often remember my family performing the "Family Role skit" for people new to the program. Our family became a spokesperson of sorts for Addiction and Rehabilitation in our community. I was no longer a dusty novelty book on the shelf; I was now front and center in every sense of the word.

My father went on to sponsor many people in

Alcoholics Anonymous (AA). My mother was a Tough-Love facilitator who helped train in Boston, Massachusetts, and facilitated groups in Brighton, Michigan. She chaired Alateen and Alanon meetings, then devoted the remainder of her career working with at-risk youth by taking them to Pip-Fest or OMIAC conventions. My mom also founded alternative education programs for at-risk children to help them finish school and is now a leader for Celebrate Recovery.

My mother made a very respected name for herself in our community. But this didn't come from an easy path. There were many bumps and twisty turns on the way. It was an uphill battle for sure.

My father retired from Ford and maintained his sobriety until the day he was called Home. At his passing, he had just celebrated 27 years of sobriety.

I know that many mistakes were made with everyone along the way, some worse than others. Looking back at my childhood, I can honestly say that my parents failed our family in one way. When I say "failed," I will also say it was not "intentional." They did not raise us in a home of faith. Therefore, one huge difference is that I had no foundation in a religious belief because I was not brought up with one.

The foundation of our home was chaos and addiction. This caused trauma in our lives. Life was unpredictable, and we became conditioned to living in chaos. When I talk about chaos in our lives, it is often not the kind that can be seen.

Even with the amount of dysfunction that took place, I can't help but think that it might have held the house up a little better had the foundation been stronger. It was a slam dunk case of generational failure in how we were raised because of how my parents were raised.

My parents did everything they could to rectify addiction issues in our home, and they succeeded in many ways. I can one-hundred percent, without any uncertainty, state that my parents did the best they could with the tools they had in their shed at the time.

I can honestly say that my family was put through hell. Between my father's addiction and sobriety, then the family dynamic.

Their love story is something that, to this day, I admire greatly. I can honestly say that I was protected from much of what took place. For that, I am thankful. I never understood it back then. Today I am healthy enough to understand it completely.

Back then, I felt like a novelty book on the shelf that was only removed when needed or to be shown off.

Looking back, I think that although I was often in the back seat of the chaos taking place, I know that the times that my mother would pick me up and head to a spur of the moment movie, have a sleepover with her friends, or the times I was sent places to hang out, it was out of necessity to protect me from what was taking place in the home.

My mom and dad would then work together to get things calmed down, then I would return. I was bitter about this for a long time growing up.

If you ask my brothers their opinions and memories of our environment growing up, they are vastly different than my memories. I believe this is because I was that book that my mother put on a shelf. I am thankful for that today; it protected me from so much.

I know that this is something that haunts my mother today. She speaks about it often when she does her open talks. In her opinion, it was part of the family dysfunction. I agree with that as well. But weirdly, it also was my protection from so much more than just being that book on the shelf. It's ironic how feelings change when you begin to follow a Christ-like life. When I was younger, the surface was anger and being bitter with this concept. My adult Christian self can change my perspective and look at it positively. Pastor Paul always says "If you can't change your circumstances, change your perspective." Today, I am thankful that my mother had the shelf to put that book on, but I'm also grateful that she chose to do that, because in reality, it protected me from many things.

CHAPTER FIVE
DESTRUCTION OF LITTLE FAITH

I was very blessed with the fact that I was extremely close with my grandparents. I spent most weekends with them. My mother was an excellent planner. Although I enjoyed the time immensely with my grandparents on the farm, especially the horses, I never really knew what might be taking place back home. I know many times I was sent there due to what was happening. I believe that did work out for my benefit because I adored spending time with my grandparents.

Around age nine, I got my first taste of faith. My best friend growing up, Jamie, and I began going to the Peoples Church in Pinckney, Michigan. They had a program called "Awanas." A teacher of ours had invited me from school named Mrs. T. My mother dropped us off each week at 6:00 pm and picked us up at 8:00 pm.

We began with singing worship, then had a short bible study, then my favorite was game time and snack. Sounds fun, right? It was a highlight of both Jamie's and my week. I was looking forward to it

From Darkness to Light

each day. Then one Wednesday during game time a boy approached me by the name of Thomas. He was a bit older and was the son of one of the youth leaders. He had older siblings who knew my brothers. He began teasing me about my home life and what he had heard was taking place. I remember this day and the words spoken.

"Angela, you shouldn't be here; God doesn't like people like you or want you here."

My friend Jamie stood up for me, which was hard for her to do as she did not like conflict of any kind. She was the type who would run the other way if any conflict was presented to her.

Today this would change. It was a day when she decided to stand up to someone bullying me about something that I had zero control over.

She stepped in between Thomas and me and said, "Don't talk to her like that, Thomas." He raised his hand to her and knocked her down to the ground in the gymnasium where we played games. His mother, the youth leader, walked over to us and said, "You girls, run along and stop messing around." We attempted to tell her what her son had done, but she shooed us away. We had done nothing wrong at this point.

It was nearing the end of the night, and as Jamie

and I were walking out, Thomas walked up behind us and stepped on the heels of the back of my brand-new white reebok tennis shoes. As I turned, he smirked at us and said,

"It's about time you go because no one wants you here."

I raised my foot off the ground, pulled my leg back, and kicked him square in the private parts, then turned and walked away.

As I got into the car with Jamie, I remember looking back and seeing him leaning over, holding himself in the doorway. Later my mother received a call stating that both Jamie and I were asked not to return to Awanna's program for inappropriate behavior. Yes, you read that correctly, two young girls got themselves kicked out of church.

To this day, I am not fully aware if my family knows the whole story of this. When they read it in this book, it may be the first time anyone other than Jamie and Thomas hear of this.

In my opinion, at that young age, I felt the church and faith were a lie and judgmental. I believed that the church leaders allowed the pain to be inflicted among the children.

Again, I was young and didn't have a grasp on what took place. I was likely judged because of the reputation that my family had. Although, yes, my behavior and retaliation were inappropriate. If this is what going to Church was like, I wanted nothing to do with it.

Looking back, I know that this was only one family in the church, a child and his mother. It was not the actual body of the church, but that's my now self, not my then child self. Had I told my mother the truth of what happened this day, she would have handled this situation appropriately. I didn't at the time feel I could bring this to her. She had too many other things going on.

My distaste for religion quickly became an issue during the time I spent at my grandparents' house.

My grandparents went to church every Sunday, and on the weekends when I stayed with them, I went also. The church they attended honestly scared me a bit back then. It was a Pentecostal church that did things quite a bit differently. Since then, I have learned the difference in the churches. I am not saying that the Pentecostal faith is bad. My oldest niece Niccole and my daughter Alexys attend a Pentecostal church.

I had a bad experience as a child at the church my grandparents attended. I remember people praying over me as a young child and feeling like something was wrong with me. One time I was in the middle of a group of people who seemed to be speaking a foreign language. As they were touching me, I recall feeling scared. No one explained to me what was taking place. I began laughing and wondering what in the heck were they saying and what was wrong with me.

Full disclosure, I am the type of person who laughs when someone gets hurt or at the most inappropriate times. Not because it is funny; that is just my armor. I get this from my mother actually.

My grandfather was so upset with me that day. I didn't get my cinnamon ice cream treat from Bill Knapp's. Back then, this was a big deal to me.

I remember another time being counseled alone by the pastor and him saying, "Little Angela Marie, come sit here with me so we can talk," as he patted his lap, which I thought was very weird. Nothing wrong ever happened. It just did not feel right to me.

I never told my grandparents about this behavior. In speaking to my grandfather about this recently, he never suspected or knew. In fact, he found out in my previous book when he read it. I had just assumed he knew. I was wrong.

Looking back as an adult, I feel like I was being groomed. At that point, I decided I did not like religion or believe in God. My viewpoint was, "If faith feels like this, I don't want it."

I have never grasped the reasons for the behaviors I witnessed; I just knew it was not for me. I still, at that time, did not understand the word Faith. I now realize that they were speaking in tongues, which was a gift. But that was not my cup of tea at the time. This negative experience was now strike three on my journey of faith.

In one experience, I was not protected by the youth leader when her son was belittling and bullying me, or physically assaulting my best friend, Jamie. Once I defended myself, I was expelled from that program.

In the second experience, I was put into a circle surrounded by adults from the church. They were touching me, speaking in tongues, and praying over me. This scared me, and I thought something was wrong with me. I was very young and had no clue what was taking place.

In another experience, I was being groomed for something that would only end in trauma. I am very thankful that nothing inappropriate ever happened. But this was strike three. If this is what Church, God, and Faith look like, NO, THANK YOU.

Can you, as a reader, imagine having those experiences in faith and then being sent to a Catholic School? I can because it happened to me.

I did not willingly go to a Catholic school; I was sent there not because I was Catholic but because I was failing miserably in our public school system. I was beginning to leave a trail of mass destruction. I was failing, skipping, and about to fail entirely in my junior year. It was not necessarily by choice; it was out of necessity to graduate and walk across a stage.

Little did I know that the stage would be in a church where communion was given before getting my diploma.

If I could go back and change this, I would not. I learned more academics in one year there than I did in three years attending public school.

The one thing that I did NOT learn was how to walk with God. I still wanted nothing to do with Faith, Church, or God. I was the student in Theology class that was negotiating theories to disbar what our teacher was lecturing and educating us on. Looking back on this, I was such a fool. I am happy that my Theology instructor was a good Christian man because I am sure that he often wanted to chuck an eraser at me.

One thing I can say without any reservation is this: the lack of a faith foundation in our home shaped me not to have any faith, then add in the three strikes in my younger years. It was a lost cause. It is tragic if you look back on it all.

The reality of it all is this; my childhood made my next steps in faith an easy choice at that time. I am not blaming my childhood; it just made the transition into Witchcraft too easy.

Everything in my life at that point felt like I was being rejected or made me feel like something was wrong with me. So, hey, let's begin practicing Witchcraft, right? That sounded like a great idea at the time.

CHAPTER SIX
THE RINK

It's a Supersonic Friday, the kind of Friday spent on those pink painted skates you read about previously. The music playing was one of my favorite songs to skate to, Supersonic by J.J. Fad.

It was the perfect roller-skating song, especially taking those corners with the line behind you as you lead them to the next corner, with the little skating routine to follow. Nothing like watching a long line of people all in sync skating and dancing to a song. It was especially good when you were leading the line, because if someone accidentally fell it was like a train derailment. If you have ever lined up dominoes, then pushed them down you will understand what this might look like.

LYRICS of Supersonic

"We're J.J. Fad and we're here to rock Rhymes like ours could never be stopped see, there's three of us and I know we're fresh Party rockers, non-stoppers, and our names are def.

See, the "J" is for "just"

The other for "jammin'"

The "F" is for "fresh" "A" and "D," "def"

Behind the turntables is DJ Train Mixin' and scratchin' is the name of the game Now here's a little somethin' 'bout nosy people It's not real hard, it's plain and simple Baby-D Supersonic Supersonic."

This was my every Friday and Saturday growing up. My mom would drop my friend Jamie and me off at the rink. We always met longtime friends Lloyd, Jack, Amy, and Donavan there. Mom would run some errands and then come back to pick us up after the third session.

Being a member of the speed skating team, I spent multiple days there during the week as well, training for upcoming meets. It was harmless and safe fun for us until it wasn't anymore.

I ended up getting a job there, working the concession stand, and being a floor guard. This was a great time and a fun job. Most of us working there were teenagers, just getting our licenses. It indeed was one of the funnest jobs that I had. At that time, many of us kids put our heart and soul into working there, as it was the "In place to work."

It was innocent fun; back then, it was safe for my

parents to drop us off, leave and come back to pick us up. Today I could not imagine doing this with my children, partly due to the nation today and partly due to what I know now from my past at the rink.

Let me also say that what I am about to discuss, my parents or family had no clue what was about to happen until it was too late. It is tough to leave once the "alternative" world encompasses you.

It was a Friday night, May 1st, to be exact. I remember they played the "Happy Birthday" song for me as I was working floor guard. This was a big deal for us because we got a free meal in the concession stand. Little did I know the next gift I would receive would change every ounce of my being.

They hired a new guy a couple of days prior; he was a bit older. A grown adult male, he was short, stocky, with super curly brown hair. His name was Natas, and he was hired as the new Disc Jockey. Back then, things were not computerized. They ran songs from disc and vinyl records. Natas was the one who played my birthday song that day. Cutting in on the intercom and stating, "Today is a special day for our very own speed queen Angela Rodgers, skate by and wish her a happy Beltane birthday." I assumed he made a mistake when speaking or that the music playing made his happy birthday sound differently. I had no idea what Beltane meant.

Later that night, at closing time, I was sitting in the employee lounge, which was located off the back of the skating rink; it had lockers and a bench. It wasn't anything special, but it was a place to store our things. I was sitting on the bench and taking my roller skates off, and as I was placing them in my locker, I felt the room get icy cold, which struck me strange as it was always sweltering due to the central furnace being in there.

I heard the door shut behind me, and I thought it was my friend Donavan, so I didn't even turn to see. I said, "Is it cold in here or what?" A voice I hadn't heard in that room before said, "Cold like my soul, just like I like it." I turned seeing Natas there, standing near the door. He was opening his newly assigned locker. He looked at me as he took a small two-inch purple felt drawstring bag out of his locker. He held it up by the string and handed it to me, saying "I want to wish you a happy Beltane birthday."

I opened it in awe of something so beautiful. It was a small sphere crystal with wiring wrapped around it, like a claw attached to a necklace. I offered him gracious thanks as he offered to assist me in putting it on. I can remember his hands touching my neck. They were ice cold; however, where he was touching my neck, it was hot. As he clasped the necklace behind my neck, he said these words I will never forget.

"This is my offering to you, for you, may our loyalty and fun never end so mote it be."

He repeatedly said this in a "chant-like voice" as he clasped it around my neck. I mean, what could go wrong, right? But Beltane, Who is Beltane? He said that word again, and I had no idea what or who that was.

I was just a stupid kid, although strange someone I never officially met was offering me anything, let alone a beautiful piece of jewelry. His words seemed odd, but Natas had a bizarre demeanor, so I didn't think much of it. In hindsight, there were HUGE red flags everywhere. I'm talking about the kind of flags that could land a plane on a lego or ones that could be seen from outer space.

Given the foundation that I was brought up in, I ignored those flags completely. I was getting attention from someone who knew nothing of my past or how I was brought up. He didn't know my brothers or family, and he most definitely didn't make me feel like a book on a shelf like my mother had.

What he had to offer seemed appealing to me. He carried himself with great power and respect. He commanded the same with each conversation he had with me. This is where it all began - the absolute, completely obliterated destruction of what little faith I had left.

From that day on, I began to be Nata's main project. Other girls in the rink were envious that he was paying so much attention to me. Although I still had no clue as to why. He was never flirtatious or physically inappropriate with me. He was much more dangerous to my soul.

He began grooming me for Wicca 3 to 4 days a week. Every time I went to work or practice, he was there waiting with a new lesson of sorts. We began spending quite a bit of time together. I would go into work early and leave late to accommodate his need for time with me. He started making my schedule at work to match his so that we could even have extra time. Often, he would "send me home early" to gain a few spare moments.

He made things seem like a new popular fad, a new belonging of sorts. I never questioned what he said, did, taught, and made me do. Because he had earned my trust. He never did anything to make me feel like I was doing something wrong or immoral. I mean, I bet you don't see any red flags here, right?

Looking back now, it was like a predator grooming a child for their own need. Nothing ever sexually or physically inappropriate happened between Natas and me. The need to please him and his beliefs were always at the forefront of my mind, most often coming before my own. That in itself is very inappropriate.

I never felt forced by him or made to feel that I had to follow his ways. But it was bizarre that I wanted to do as he said, I wanted to please him, and I wanted to learn more of what he was teaching.

He was able to make it a need of mine to please and follow him. I felt obligated. It is difficult to understand myself still today. He and I could communicate from across the room and know what the other was thinking with little effort or thought. If a dangerous situation came near, we knew. Once in particular, he was in a car accident, and I knew something was wrong before he even advised me what had taken place. We became a power duo at the rink, but sadly it didn't end there.

I was altogether one hundred percent at this

point, both Pagan and Wiccan. I couldn't learn enough of the Magic world and was catching on to spell casting very quickly. Although I never fell into a world of drug abuse and addiction, like my father and brothers, I did absolutely fall into addiction to Natas, Wiccan and Paganism. I was climbing the ranks quickly and became known in our surrounding area as an accomplished spellcaster and powerhouse of energy. I quickly became addicted and consumed to all things that involved Magic and the power that came with it.

During this time, I had a lot of time to dabble into magic, this wasn't a good scenario. By this time, I had already jumped headfirst into rituals, spells, and circle work. I was performing and writing my own spells some of which were beneficial and some of which were harmful. I was working spells on people, animals, and nature. I was practicing rituals both by myself and within a circle. I was part of Satan's team; I opened my life to it and invited it in. I was actively engaging in the forces of darkness. I was connecting Satan and his demons, and nothing could be more dangerous. Initially, it seemed benign, even innocent. The Bible says Satan positions himself as an angel of light, but then the evil engulfs you. It is more than playing with fire. It's dousing yourself with gasoline and then sparking the match. **IT IS**

SPIRITUAL SUICIDE.

In many areas I was feared and in other areas I was put on a pedestal. This was interesting to me because I was just a teenage girl. It appeared that I once again was that book on a shelf that was dusted off and used only when needed.

I was now known as Trinity, the youngest of a very powerful Coven of thirteen. I was just waiting to ask permission to take my spot as the leader and High Priestess of my very own. I just had to make it to the prerequisite one year and a day.

I am sure some of you are asking yourself, "How did my parents not know this was going on?" Keep reading because that blowout is in the very next chapter. Looking back as my adult self, I'm still in absolute awe of the grace that was given to me when I absolutely did not deserve it.

By grace, I do mean from the Lord Jesus Christ. Also, from my mother and father who I am quite sure wanted to kick my ass multiple times during this journey. I don't know if it would have made much of a difference, because I was consumed in something much bigger than myself or the foundation that my parents had given me.

CHAPTER SEVEN
MEETING NATAS

To say my parents noticed, changes in my behavior is an understatement. Even with those changes causing concern, it still wasn't enough red flags for them to intervene. We did have a few conversations regarding their concerns. At that point, they were likely just thinking I was on drugs. My mom asked me multiple times, and I said I wasn't doing any drugs; I wasn't. It was much worse.

I remember walking into the door the evening I got my necklace. I walked up to my mom to show her while she was on the phone with a family who needed rehabilitation for their teen. She looked at me and smiled but didn't say too much. When she got off the phone, she stated that she wasn't a big fan of it. But she didn't inquire with any questions or concerns at that time. This didn't last long.

A few months later, I was having a slumber party one night. I decided to play with some Magic, not the WIGI board or the Light as a feather type of Magic. However, we did play with that as well. The Magic I decided to toy with this evening was a ritual with my and my girlfriend's blood drops. I created a circle in the middle of my bedroom and did a bonding spell. At this point, I was utterly consumed and actively practicing daily.

I began speaking openly about Natas to my family and friends. Once I started doing this, my wise mother was on me like our dog Cory was on my brother's drug stashes.

Can you believe that my mother decided to go and sit in the concession area of the skating rink the very next Friday? She knew something was going on. My mother didn't know that I was sitting in the back room with Natas spell casting, when my friend Lloyd busted in and said, "Your mom is here with Kevin, and she is looking for you." It surprised me when she walked in to "check" on me and what was going on. Bringing my brother was just a bonus. My mom, my brother, nicknamed Bam Bam, myself, and my mind manipulator all together; what could go wrong?

I walked out of the back room with Natas flanking alongside Lloyd. Asking her what she was doing here, she simply said calmly, "Just here checking in on you." What I didn't miss was her sideways look to my right at Natas, then looking back to my brother Kevin, then to me. Natas smiled, or more of a smirk, as he decided it would be a great time to have a pissing contest with "Bam Bam" himself. I could hear Lloyd standing directly beside me mumbling under his breath saying, "O man, this is going to be bad."

As Nata's turned to walk away from us, he stopped, looked back over his right shoulder to me and said, "Are you coming?" as he raised his eyebrow, pointing to the ground at his right side with his index finger. I must say this was not a great choice for him to make at that time. I got pretty concerned quickly; I felt the "mom look" I was getting from my mother and felt the change in attitude from my brother. I knew this was going to erupt quickly. I looked at Kevin and said, "No Don't." When I said that, Natas turned and said something under his breath, to this day I don't know what that was. The next thing I knew, Kevin had Nata's jacked up against the wall between the bathroom and drinking fountain by his throat. I remember Natas being shocked as his feet left the floor. My mother said calmly, "Kevin put him down." My brother literally dropped him and walked away. They went and just sat in the Concession area. Of course, I went on about my business, staying out of the back room.

I mean, whose mother would dare come to a place where they suspected something was going on, check on her child, and bring my hotheaded television throwing brother, to jack my mind manipulator up against the wall? My mom and I would do it today in a hot minute.

The next day I woke up, and Mom wanted to talk with me, a family meeting with just my mother and me. She never once asked me what was going on. She sat and waited in silence. I told her everything that she didn't ask with just a few short words "Mom, give him a chance; you can meet him and talk to him if you want." That was the 'in' she wanted; well played, Mom.

She agreed, and I planned the meeting at the local Big Boy. We were going to sit down and have dinner together. I mean, what could go wrong? My mother wanted to speak to my Coven leader about the changes she noticed and what was happening to her daughter. At least she didn't bring my hot-headed brother.

Walking into Big Boy, I am not sure who was more nervous, myself or my mother. I know that Natas was complaisant because nothing could touch him in his world. We sat at the table over coffee in silence for much of the time.

My mother began asking the normal questions,

Age, job and family status. He was obliged to answer all her questions. Then he struck a nerve with her. He began speaking of my father and about his recent health issues. He was doing it to demonstrate to my mother the level of control he had over me and my mind. Planting the seed that there was something wrong with my father while sitting at the table with my mother was over the top, but it worked.

Again, my mother, although very skeptical, played along. I can tell you that this became the most awkward meeting to date that I have ever had.

After this "meeting" ended, I left with my mother, who wasn't saying too much. I think perhaps she may have been afraid due to the level of control he had over me at this time.

As a parent now, I can imagine the horror in her mind. She didn't know that I was biding my time for my 366th day. I had a bigger plan myself; I was waiting for the day I could implement it.

To this day, I do not know why she didn't forbid me from seeing him. At this point, I assumed that she was aware of what was taking place. I made no secret of my distaste for religion, and she was smart enough to notice the sage in my room, salt in my closet, and the quickly multiplying number of crystals I had attained.

I recently asked my mother her version of why she handled this situation the way she did back then. I had never asked her before. Much to my surprise, she answered with this, "I didn't know. In all honestly, you weren't doing drugs and that was my main concern at that time. I figured if you weren't doing drugs, it couldn't be that bad." She went on to explain that at that point and time in our lives the drug use was the primary concern of hers.

I'm sure that looking back now, her viewpoint would be different. We can't go back and change what happened then. But having this conversation with my mother did "check" me on a couple of parental things I have also done.

CHAPTER EIGHT
DOWNSLIDE INTO WICCA

Wicca, like anything else, has multiple components. Each person's take on those components will be different from the next. I will not tell you that what I was taught was correct. In that, it means what I taught others was incorrect. I am here to tell you NEVER DO WHAT I DID. It was wrong and had very grave consequences.

I am sure of one thing: I was taught from someone who intended to use me as a weapon. So, therefore I know my story will be much different than those of you who are reading this - especially those who have experienced lessons in witchcraft.

My recruitment into Wicca happened over time. I did not even know what was taking place in the beginning. That's not an excuse, but that is a fact. By the time I realized what was happening, it was too late. I was hooked on the evolving power, no matter how dark that became.

There are three typical degrees in Wicca, each

takes work to get through, but typically it is working at your own pace. Natas had a plan, so things moved along quicker for me than most.

I unknowingly made a Sigil into Wicca. Sigils are tiny seeds of desire and intent that can blossom in our minds only if we plant them. We plant them by making sigils, visualizing, and activating them.

First-Degree Wiccans are required to learn the basics of Wicca. This degree is meant to give you a basic introduction to Wicca. I am focusing on the traditional signs and symbols such as the Pentagram, Pentacle, Triple Goddess, Goddess, and Horned God.

I was new to working with the elements of my magic. I was doing basic spells and creating my altar space for my rituals. This was simple because I created my alter space in my bedroom at home. It wasn't anything special; it was in my closet, and I had all the items needed for my work. Everything I used blended in with my room, and questions were never asked - the things that didn't blend in with my room I simply hid from my parents.

Second-degree Wiccans are required to learn advanced Wiccan practices. The second-degree carries a responsibility to the Craft as a whole. Once granted the degree, you may guest with other covens or attend other classes of different witchcraft traditions. During second-degree work, I could explore practices by myself without supervision.

I faced some challenges dealing with some of the advanced spell work, not because I was terrible at it. But because it was never enough. The typical dream, rituals, and short spells bored me, and I wanted more. I was a Wicca addict, and enough was never enough.

Third-degree Wiccans are just witches who can understand Wicca well enough to debate and create theology intelligently. Once you reach the third-degree, you can teach your personal coven. Third-degree recruits must be mystical, magical, and spiritual experts, and have the skill set to prepare information for lower-level Wiccans.

Yes, you read that right; as a third-degree witch, I was able to create my own form of theology. Today, my Christian-self rubs my temples when I think of this. Only by the grace of God am I still here today.

I was a rarity in this as I completed all these steps and asked for evaluation on day 366. In many Wiccan traditions, it is customary for someone to study for a year and a day before being formally initiated. In some cases, the standard length of time must pass between degree levels once the person is initiated into the group.

Although the year and the day rule for initiates are most found in Wicca and NeoWicca, it occasionally appears in other Pagan paths.

For many Pagans and Wiccans, the year-and-a-day study period holds a special significance. This time is so you and the group's other members can get to know one another. It's also a time in which you can familiarize yourself with the concepts and principles of the group. This rule was supposed to allow me to be part of an established tradition and enable me to give my practice structure. Some witches choose to study for this time before any self-dedication ritual. But not me at that time.

By the year mark, I had already in my mind built my coven. I just needed the initiation to be able to have permission to do so. I got that and began.

CHAPTER NINE
WITCHCRAFT 101

Know that this chapter is hard to write because I in no way, shape, or form wish to entice a person to want to learn about witchcraft. It is the last thing I want to do.

I now know that there is only one God to worship and that all the false idols that witchcraft idolizes are a sin. When my day comes, I will have to answer for my prior life's choices. I am entirely okay with that fact. I know who I am today, and I know that I screwed up. ROYALLY.

I can only hope that the life I live now is enough to right my wrongs on my day of judgment. When I meet my Maker, when HE decides to bring me home, I hope to hear the words "Well Done, Angela, Well Done." If I could go back in time and change the decisions of Witchcraft I made, I absolutely would.

But given the foundation I was not given as a child, and the foundation I was being offered, combined with the few negative experiences I had in faith, I didn't know any better. I would do anything to be able to reverse the clock to that first day of May when I was a child. I would have never allowed Natas to place a necklace upon my neck. I would have never allowed him to touch me at all. I would have read the room better when it changed temperature from blazing hot to freezing cold.

I WOULD HAVE LEFT AND HAD A BOUNDARY THERE LARGER THAN THE ATLANTIC OCEAN.

But I was young and dumb, so this did not happen. A simple day in the life of a teenage girl living the dream. Working in a skating rink. An uprising star on the speed team and an all-around good kid. This changed with the click of a simple metal clasp placed around my neck. To this day, I have issues with being touched. I am very much a this is my space, and this is your space kind of person. People ask me before they hug me because they know I have issues with being touched.

A functioning witch is not a person who has the primary focus of "self-improvement." I can hear those "new age" wheels turning with a few of you. Just put that idea out of your head. A witch is not a witch to serve only themselves. Period. There is always something more significant.

Wicca, as of 1986, is classified as a true religion. I

will speak more on this later. Its supporters call themselves "witches" and their religious practices "witchcraft," but those terms in that context are specific to Wicca. Some began calling themselves witches as a feminist statement. It marked them as nothing more than a rebel who may or may not be Wiccan or doing any actual witchcraft. Others have said they were witches, just for notoriety and the ahh haa responses. For the rest of the known world, a conscious witch has meant someone wielding energy and knowledge to affect their environment, including the people around them.

People have the thought process of what they view as stereotypical witches. Most think that they are people who fly around on brooms with pointed hats, wear cloaks, and have very dark personalities. I have heard some use the words "dark and gothic and covered with crystals." Most don't know that although some of these things are possible, you're likely not even to know you are near someone practicing magic. They could be your Aunt, Uncle, Local Judge, business owner, or Attorney. In my case, I was a regular-looking teenage girl who was also a daughter, granddaughter, and sister.

Some witches are going to be self-serving in that. But even the most selfish and egotistical witch has some sort of understanding that they need a circle, which may or may not include humans.

There are some very inhumane and ruthless witches as well. They tend to form a dirty and dark bubble around themselves, full of nothing but minions and nasty energy gained through traumatizing others. I honestly believe that this is more how Natas operated, thus the reason that I chose to stay in the "broom closet" for so long. It was a legitimate choice I had made, due to the way I was taught. Even when I decided to come out of the "broom closet," I still had to be very careful with things I said, something I did, things that I had done, and lastly, things I had planned on doing.

I had a very strong will. When I said I was a strong-willed child, this was an understatement. With that being said, I was dangerous in witchcraft, which often made me a target of spiritual warfare. I quickly realized that I was not the only person with a strong will. I then learned that I needed to be careful about attracting too much ill will. Not just the ill will of other practicing witches but the ill will of people in general. Many people do not like witches, and some actively attempt to combat or thwart efforts.

In my coven, I had multiple people who disapproved of what I was doing or working on at the moment. But not one of them challenged me at the time, much due to my will or fear. You are taught not to question your leader. I made that mistake a couple of times with Natas.

One of the most important things I had to learn as a witch was to keep my mouth shut. Anyone who personally knows me know this was a miracle. I am a very blunt and direct person; I have never been one to hold anything back or not say what is on my mind. I had to learn that not everybody needed to know that I was a witch, and not everyone who knew I was a witch needed to know the specifics of my workings.

The more people who knew your witchcraft business, the more possibility of being attacked. People could attack or thwart me out of fear, some out of jealousy, and some because of other personal interests. Regardless, I was always up for a good challenge, but I didn't always seek it out.

Interestingly enough, some church leaders nowadays operate in a like way, in my opinion, now, as a devout Christian. Pastors, Priests, and Minister's keep clients' confidence and other people they serve. Much like clergy today in most "conventional religions," I did the same in witchcraft. It goes a little farther than clergy, though, because even telling some people ABOUT what I was doing caused a bad reaction that could ruin my work. I was cautious with who I shared things with, even my blessings. Some people may hear your news and give you the evil eye or envious energy in return.

I plan to speak more on this in later chapters. Because sadly, there is so much evil and ugliness that revolves around Witchcraft, Luciferians, and Satanists, that most of you wouldn't believe it. It is all one big circle of people worshiping something dangerous. I know because I was one of them.

CHAPTER TEN
THE RECRUITMENT

To understand the process of my recruitment you need first to understand what I had become in this practice. In the essence of destroying myself, I destroyed others as well. I believe that I was taught incorrectly, in fact, in a way that was self-serving to Natas. In the end, I was able to identify and find out that he was not only Pagan and Wicca but also a Luciferian. This hurts me because this shaped my sense of belonging in all areas of my life.

A High Priestess is a woman who leads a Coven or a Wiccan ritual. So, she will be very knowledgeable about Wicca and Witchcraft. But there is so much more to it. In Wicca, every practitioner is a Priestess or Priest.

The primary difference between a priestess and a High Priestess is the knowledge, experience, desire, and ability to give of herself in Wicca. Also, to be of service to others and the Divine, which revolves around a Goddess and a Horned God, thereby being generally dualistic. Does this sound like Satanism to you? It sure does to me.

High Priestesses have responsibilities. You become a High Priestess by the performance, not just by choosing the title. It was a lot of work. The amount of time I spent proving myself to people who were worshiping someone other than the one true God disgusts me. I still get a pit in my stomach when I think of this.

To fulfill the responsibilities of a High Priestess, you needed to be familiar with the basics of the craft, and fluently skilled in the following:

~Advanced Wicca

~Magic and energy work

~Organization

~Planning Wiccan rituals

~Event coordination

~Management

~People skills

~Conflict Resolution

~Ritual etiquette

~Teaching others

~Channeling and Aspecting the Divine

There are also personality requirements for this

role. Not everyone is cut out for it. Like being the president or an elected official, the people most qualified for the job often don't want it, and the unqualified people are eager for it.

Most people only notice the glamour and what looks like the power of the position. They overlook the hard work and tireless dedication that comes with the job. They also don't notice that the leader is the one who is serving the Coven or Circle, not the one wielding power. This was one of many things that Natas taught me inaccurately.

Recruitment for my coven was not done per the "book" per'se. Vastly, due to the fact of how I was taught and partly due to the fact I had already built my coven before being allowed to. While I was learning from Natas, I already had my eyes set on who would be standing next to me.

It is said that Wicca does not recruit at all, that those who choose to be a part of it get to. Fortunately, this is not the case entirely. I was recruited, so I recruited; I made it look fun and powerful to do so.

My first recruit was Lloyd, who was easy given he was one of my oldest childhood friends, beginning at age 9. He had been by my side during most of my training with Natas, so it seemed natural, but I didn't stop there. I then found Donavan,

Noelle, Sarah, Marie, Amy, Patrick, Hope, Misty, Koda, Chad, Greg, and last but certainly not least, Christine.

The one thing I did not expect to have was a soul tie with Lloyd, this complicated things along the way. In many cases, it is said that a soul tie comes into existence after two people have been physically intimate. In others, it is said to form after an intensely close spiritual or emotional relationship.

Lloyd and I had the latter of the two. It was never physically intimate, but that soul tie was strong from our spiritual and emotional relationship. He and I were very close. I spent a lot of time at his house with his family. He was brought up Catholic but was not a practicing one. We did have the same belief in religion and our distaste for it. I never hurt Lloyd. I was protective of him to a fault. That word got around quickly when we were younger, so interestingly enough, he could never practice like many others. This made me angry back in the day, but today, I believe it was God's divine intervention.

When I look back at the number of lives that were impacted and hurt by my actions and that of my coven, it makes me physically sick.

One specific story was with Lloyd and Christine;

they gained a soul tie of their own in the form of intimacy and a spiritual and emotional relationship. They were together for many years.

Unintentionally, we found Christine in a moment of weakness and despair; she was unhappily married with two children. I wanted to recruit her, and Lloyd tried to court her. This caused some issues with Lloyd and me. Relationships in a coven are complicated. Relationships in a coven where there is a previous soul tie are impossible.

Ultimately, Christine left her then-husband, divorced, and followed the path. This is my second biggest regret in my responsibilities as High Priestess in my craft. First was getting involved in it at all.

Christine was brought up with a great family and in a Christian home. Her parents were the fairy tale marriage that most children would dream of, in fact, still are. I had met a lot of her family, and in general, they were beautiful, gracious people and devout Christians. They gave her the foundation in Christ before I showed her a foundation in Satanic ways.

If any of you are reading this, I am sorry. Forgive me for showing your beautiful daughter, sister, mom, wife, and aunt the dark side of Magic. I am so thankful that she found her way back to the light and has risen above so much in her life. In my opinion, she is the epitome of love and forgiven grace.

I know I am not to blame for the demise of their marriage; however, I am responsible for my part in pulling her to the dark side of magic, as I saw fit in a moment of her weakness. This was my fault, and I take one hundred percent responsibility. I have often thought that she could have possibly fixed her marriage and her family had I not pulled her into the craft. That is an answer I will never know. She and I have spoken on this previously as well.

I had nothing to do with the soul tie between her and Lloyd. However, I did not discourage it; I played a supportive role.

Lloyd and I are still great friends today; our soul tie is also healthy. Both of us are happily married and no longer have the spiritual or emotional relationship we had. He no longer practices Magic; it is why he and I can be friends today. We don't talk every day, but we check in with each other. He is someone I can always count on in a time of need. It took him and me many years to become healthy friends, but if you want something bad enough, you work at it, even if it doesn't come easy.

Christine and I went our separate ways for a long time, years in fact. She and Lloyd ended their relationship after many years. I can say that I am blessed with the forgiveness that Christine has shown me.

It was not easily given; it was very much undeserved. I had to prove myself and work for that.

It took a separation from us for her to find herself again. I was a toxic person in my path at that time. Christine knew I was my father's baby girl, and she also knew that it would test every ounce of my being when he died. He had been very ill for a long time, but I assume when he finally had his "final homecoming," she wanted to see how I would handle it. When my father passed away, she contacted my mother and brother for condolences. She never contacted me, and I completely understand why. She didn't trust what I might do in that situation and knew I needed to find my way.

I can now say that she is one of my Jesus Sisters in Christ; we are both Christians in faith and friends. She is a beautiful soul inside and out. She is a blessing to me, and I will never violate that trust with her again.

Both her and Lloyd were very supportive when I approached them for their blessing in writing this story. I think they have seen the growth in me and trust me - that is a blessing in itself.

CHAPTER ELEVEN
THE BAD, WORSE AND UGLY

Before my young self-lit candles on the small altar in my bedroom closet each night, I said my "witchy" prayers: "Hail, fair Moon, ruler of the night, guard me and mine until the light. Hail fair Sun, ruler of the day, make the morn to light my way." On my altar are four porcelain chalices representing the elements - air, water, fire, and earth. Each contained rose petals, stones, melted candle wax, and dried leaves. They rest on the corners of a five-pointed star. A frog symbolizing "spirit" and "life" sits on point five of the pentagram. Here, I often performed rituals and cast spells before my altar.

I was one of the growing number of teenage girls who practiced Wicca. If you drive to the mall, you will see cars with bumper stickers declaring, "The goddess is alive. Magic is afoot!" Flip on the television or go to the movies, and you'll find witches portrayed as young, powerful, and glamorous.

SOMETHING IS DEFINITELY "GOING ON" IN AMERICAN CULTURE.

From TV shows to movies and even children's cartoons, something is definitely "going on" in the world today, and it is not good. Don't even get me started with the evil I see with many governments' officials, temples, or lodges. The number of hidden or corrupt things in these entities would disgust you.

For my Christian self, it is hard to understand or fathom that this takes place. Had I not lived it and done these things myself, I might not believe it. I am only disclosing and writing on less than 25% of what I have seen and done. I will lay it out there if you choose to read about it in a chapter at the end of this book because it is just that: EVIL.

One thing I can attest to is that the thought of being able to control spiritual forces sounded pretty good to me. Growing up, I felt powerless over so many things, both in my home and out of it.

Wiccans boast that their religion gives even young witches a great deal of control. Also, the secrecy of rituals may provide a sense of power. What isn't appealing about that in a young mind?

Wicca has no specific set rules or absolute standards. This is illustrated by "The Wiccan Rede," which tells followers to "do what you will." In Wicca, everyone gets to decide on their own rules. As a Wiccan high priestess, I had the rule, "Within the circle, there are no absolutes, no rights, and no wrongs."

There was only one rule besides the "Wiccan Rede," which I remember, but I was never taught about it by Natas. I learned about the "Three-fold rule" the hard way. Also known as "The Rule of Three," the Three-fold Law is part of most Wiccan traditions. It states that every magical act sent out into the Universe, whether positive or negative, will be returned to the Witch three times.

This is somewhat like the concept of karma found in some religions, but with a witchy twist, as it applies a specific equation ("three times") to the return of the energy sent out by the practitioner.

Just what did "three times" mean? Some people believe that the magical work will be returned in three individual instances. For example, I worked a harmful spell against someone I disliked. I then ended up experiencing lousy luck on three different occasions: my car broke down, I ended up in the hospital with a broken bone, and my mother ended up hospitalized with a blood clot. Others interpret "three times" as a multiplier, meaning that the consequences for you will be three times stronger than the intention you sent out. So, you might end up with far worse luck than car trouble.

The origins of the Three-fold Law are a bit murky and as clear as mud. Wicca can appear to be the perfect mix 'n' match religion. It was a free for all, to suit whatever was taking place at any given time, no matter the consequences.

Unfortunately, though these things may sound good, they're deceptions that lead followers down a path to destruction. Some deceptions are in direct conflict with the Bible and the word of Christ. I have studied both. I'm a rarity in that I'm still here to discuss the vast similarities and differences.

Wiccans worship "the mother goddess" and her companion, "the horned god." They say both deities manifest themselves in nature. For instance, my prayer acknowledged the sun as the female goddess and the moon as the god. You may also have heard the goddess referred to as Mother Nature. Wiccans believe that the goddess is in everything: rocks and trees, earth, and sky.

Sometimes, the goddess is represented by specific female deities such as the ancient Greek goddesses Artemis (the goddess of the wilderness) or

Gaia (the goddess of the Earth). Some Wiccans even claim that the goddess is Mary, the mother of Jesus. The horned god is often represented by the lusty Greek god Pan, or the Egyptian god of the dead, Osiris.

Magic and spellcasting are an integral part of Wicca. Wiccans say that spells are symbolic acts performed in an altered state of consciousness to cause the desired change. There are spells to overcome loneliness, attract money, bring inner power, and bind an enemy, among others. Witches acknowledge that spells can be used to do good or harm. Wicca has no central book (like the Bible) that spells out its beliefs, so witches practice their religion differently. Some witches meet in covens or circles, while others practice alone.

According to Wicca's myths, Wicca began within earth's first civilization more than 35,000 years ago. In this culture, women ruled. Life was peaceful and prosperous, and people worshiped nature and the goddess. The serene existence was supposedly shattered when male warriors invaded the nurturing female-led communities.

I added that word to Wiccans and Satanists. After all, I didn't want to lose you with that word because people aren't afraid when they hear the word Wicca, but the term Satanist is frightening. UMMM, to be candid, It's near the same.

Self-definition as witches, a belief in magic, and the use of an encircled, five-pointed star as a holy symbol, to name a few. The confusion ultimately boils down to a fundamental misunderstanding of three very different belief systems: Wicca, theistic Satanism, and atheistic Satanism.

Wiccans say that they have been fighting to overcome the oppression of a male-ruled society throughout history. Today, Wiccans claim there is a goddess revival. They say women are reclaiming their power after living under male domination for too long.

They call for women to usher in a new era of peace by throwing off the "shackles" of "male-dominated monotheistic religions" and follow the goddess again in all her forms. It's easy to see why this myth has enormous feminist appeal.

One thing I know is this: Wicca is short for Witch, Satanism has the very word Satan in it, and Satanism is not something you want to toy with. I can say this without any reservation because of how Natas taught me. I learned to toy with both.

We will speak more on Satanism, Satanic rituals, and Luciferianism later. For that chapter, you need to be armed with the whole armor of God.

CHAPTER TWELVE
QUESTIONABLE TRUTHS

In my years of practicing Wicca, there were many things I questioned. Many red flags as well; however, at that time, I didn't see them as specific red flags. It wasn't until I became a Christian and began studying the Bible that a lot of the "questionable truths" that I had in my Wicca days started to make sense. I can absolutely understand and open my mind up to different religions and different types of worship. But this doesn't come without questions.

With Wicca being recognized as a religion in 1986. A case was brought to the Supreme court stating that a Michigan prison was denying an inmate serving life in prison the right to exercise his 1st and 14th Amendments. He was denied the use of ceremonial items even after winning a landmark lawsuit. Later, a bench trial resulted in a June 1998 verdict in favor of the inmate, and he was awarded $1,000 and attorney fees of $20,000. *See Marsh v. Hawley, USDC, Marquette County, Michigan, Case No: 95-CV-285.*

Although I appreciate the right to practice a religion of my choice, I can see many things that could go wrong here, given the items that each could consider ceremonial, especially with a religion that has no boundaries. Beliefs are meant to have boundaries. If they weren't, why does the bible mention the word belief so many times? In my opinion, a church without them could be dangerous.

Wiccans and Pagans are typically polytheistic, believing in more than one deity. If you look at "god" as a job title rather than a proper name, they believe in various gods and goddesses rather than One Single God. Most Pagans and Wiccans acknowledge the existence of thousands of deities, but generally, they worship or honor only the gods of their tradition. Christian theology rebukes this calling it a sin to bow down to false idols.

Heaven and Hell.... Well, no. Much like Satan, the concept of Hell is not even on the Wiccan radar. However, a few people, typically those who have come to Wicca from a Christian background, worry about this issue. For the rest of Wiccan practices, they believe that the future of their soul does not depend on salvation or acceptance of a deity as a savior. Instead, they focus on doing good things because they know that what we do in this lifetime will echo upon us in the next. So, does this mean that there is no HELL? I would rather not take my chance and follow a Godly life because this isn't something I am interested in finding out about. The Christian faith and the bible clearly state that there is both a heaven and a hell.

Magic and spells depend on what Wiccans call a psychic link. Psychic development can involve training in divination, the attempt to obtain information about the past, present, or future by occult means, or one's psychic abilities. The Bible clearly states that divination and any other form of supernatural contact (other than prayer, of course!) are forbidden since it relies on a magical power apart from God. In other words, there is no such thing as "white magic." Magic is Magic. It's all bad because it isn't parallel to what is written in scripture.

The Bible says:

Deuteronomy 18:10-12,

"Let no one be found among you who sacrifices his son or daughter in the fire, who practices divination or sorcery, interprets omens, engages in witchcraft, or casts spells, or who is a medium or

spiritist or who consults the dead. Anyone who does these things is detestable to the Lord, and because of these detestable practices the Lord your God will drive out those nations before you."

Leviticus 19:26,

"Do not practice divination or sorcery."

In Wicca, each follower is told to "do as she wills." Their only standard is that no one should cause harm. In other words, there is no absolute truth. But this presents several problems for me. First, how can one be sure that no damage is being done? Is there any way to know all the consequences of an action? No! And aren't personal feelings a wishy-washy method of determining right and wrong?

A well-known Wiccan once said, "A thing is good for me until I feel it is not right for me." Another witch stated, "The witch's conscience must be the final arbiter." I question, what if a witch one day feels that incest or murder is the right thing to do? Is there anything to stop them? Even though most Wiccans would say that these things are wrong, they have no firm basis for saying so.

On the other hand, Christianity provides a powerful authority for denouncing racism, crime, or any other moral wrong: God's Holy character and His Word, the Bible.

The Bible says in *2 Timothy 3:16-17*,

> *"All Scripture is God-breathed and is useful for teaching, rebuking, correcting, and training in righteousness so that the man of God may be thoroughly equipped for every good work."*

Wiccans do not believe in sin as Christians do. They see sin as an outdated, constraining concept. Therefore, they see no need for God. The thought process on sin is more "We can now open new eyes and see there is nothing to be saved from, no struggle of life against the universe, no God outside the world, to be feared and obeyed." Through spiritual self-improvement, Wiccans hope to reach their equivalent of heaven, called the Summerland or the Land of Eternal Youth.

I would instead take my chance on the end game and that final big show and know where my eternity lays. Eternity means forever and ever, without end. The words "there shall be no end" and "forever" show the eternal purposes of God in the birth of Christ. THE INCARNATION WAS SERIOUS STUFF. Eternity is serious stuff. I know now that

Jesus is right for whatever is wrong, all the time, no matter what. The actual key to our Eternal Heaven is nailed to the cross.

Jesus reigns. He reigns in life, He reigns in death, He reigns in the heavens, and He reigns over all. He reigns above kingdoms, and He reigns above kings. He reigns above the darkness, every demon of hell, and He reigns above every circumstance of life.

He reigns above every sorrow of the heart, every need of the body, every choice of the will, and every emotion of the soul. He reigns with all authority, He reigns with all justice, He reigns with all righteousness, He reigns with all goodness, and He reigns with all might.

He reigns over the plans of men and the devil's schemes; He reigns over the laws of the universe and the laws of nature. He reigns over the earth, the climate, the storms at sea, and His reign and kingdom will have no end.

Many people stumble over the simplicity of the gospel, thinking they can win divine approval through their good deeds of religious efforts, they try to establish their own righteousness. But it is Jesus's work, not ours, that is the key to heaven!

Simply put, HE is the HE. We believe Jesus is the way, the truth, and the life (John 14:6). Everything we are and everything we have comes from Him and works together for His purpose.

CHAPTER THIRTEEN
WICCA FAR AND WIDE

God has made it clear that Wicca is dangerous and contradictory to Christianity. He made His creation for us to enjoy as a reflection of His character, but not to be worshiped instead of Him. Wicca may seem attractive, magical, and different, but it does not give eternal life and a relationship with God. If you choose Wicca, you cannot choose God as well because He will not tolerate the worship of anything but Himself. He is perfect and holy. Study God's Word, and you will find that a life centered on the Son of God, Jesus Christ, who gave His life for us on the Cross, is better than anything we could ever find here on earth.

The Bible tells us that no amount of good work can earn us eternal life. Through Christ alone, we are saved.

The Bible says:

> *"I am the way and the truth and the life. No one comes to the Father except through Me."*
> *(Jesus in John 14:6)*

Looking through the lens of Wicca, one has this image of what this looks like. I know this because I did as well. I had ideas of what a witch would look like from the shows that I loved to watch as a child and teenager. This image was able to plant the first seed of interest in my mind. These shows are popular and easily accessible to almost all. Check off all the shows on the following list that you have seen. What ones have your children seen?

~The Worst Witch (2017)

~Sabrina, the Teenage Witch (1996)

~Hex (2004)

~Good Witch (2015)

~Dark Shadows (1966)

~Charmed (1998)

~Bitten (2014)

~Emerald City (2017)

~The Secret Circle (2011)

~Midnight, Texas (2017)

~Witches of East End (2013)

~True Blood (2008)

~Charmed (2004)

~Shadowhunters (2016)

~Sleepy Hollow (2013)

~Once Upon a Time (2011)

~Buffy the Vampire Slayer (1997)

~Salem (2014)

~Merlin (2009)

~Chilling Adventures of Sabrina (2018)

~American Horror Story: Coven (2013)

~The Originals (2013)

~The Vampire Diaries (2009)

~Angel (1999)

~Grimm (2011)

~Game of Thrones (2011)

~Ash vs. Evil Dead (2015)

~The Addams Family (1964)

These are everyday television shows marketed to engage with the younger generations; they are written and shown to make it look cool and exciting.

There is no shortlist of famous blockbuster movies as well. Who hasn't seen these top-rated movies?

~The Wizard of Oz

~Practical Magic

~Harry Potter series

~Hocus Pocus

~Beetle Juice

~The Witches of Eastwick

Or let's even discuss Disney, which mass markets to the younger children. Yes, EVEN Disney markets witches and witchcraft to our youth.

~Twitches (2005) & Twitches Two (2007)

~The Halloweentown Movies (1998-2006)

~Maleficent (2014)

~Maleficent Two: Mistress of Evil (2019)

~Into the Woods (2014)

~Snow White and the Seven Dwarfs (1937)

~The Sword in the Stone (1963)

~The Little Mermaid (1989)

~Return to Oz (1985)

Sadly, even cartoons today that are rated G have witches in them. You are likely unintentionally implanting the images of witches and witchcraft into your children's minds and don't even know it. Remember the JUNK you allow IN Creates JUNK OUT. What you SEE and believe is what you are ingesting in your brain. That influences what you think and changes your behavior.

~Scooby Doo has a Witch named Sarah Ravencroft

~Duck Tales has a Witch named Magica De Spell

~The sword and the Stone has shapeshifters named Madam Mim and Merlin

~The little mermaid has a Witch named Ursula

~Sleeping Beauty has a Witch named Maleficient

~Mary and the Witches Flower has a Witch named Mary

~Snow White and the Seven Dwarfs has a Witch known as the evil queen

~The Owl House has a cursed witch named Eda

Are you asking why I am telling you this yet? It's pretty simple...

IF YOU DON'T TEACH YOUR CHILDREN TO FOLLOW CHRIST, THE WORLD WILL TEACH THEM NOT TO.

I failed at this with my older children; I speak more of this in the next chapter.

Why are movies, television, and magazines so obsessed with Wicca and witchcraft? Why do we as parents allow this implanting of Satanic images in our children? And why are teens, especially girls, so enthusiastic about picking up the trend? Nothing is safe anymore, or was it ever, to begin with? The indirect influence of witches in our culture today has existed for years. Now fast-forward to the 21st century, where witchcraft has become more persistent and often darker. From movies like "The Craft" to television shows such as "Charmed" and "Once upon a time," today's culture is saturated with witchcraft and pushes agendas and interest in Wicca and Satanism.

If you view old TV programs made 50 years ago of families relating to one another, they look like today's ideal Christian homeschool family. Daddy is respected and honored, and Mother is cherished. Family problems were always resolved with good cheer and forgiveness. Teenage morality was taken for granted. The future was bright and full of hope, and there was no state of rebellion in the kids.

In contrast, modern TV and movies usually represent today's average family - accurately, I might add - as dysfunctional psycho wards of vindictive anger and disrespect. In most movies, the family is already divorced or going through a painful process. If a movie was made with a teenager loving his parents as they love their children and each other, and everyone with good cheer and hope for the future, it would be considered corny and unrealistic to the point that the only people who could relate to it would be the ones who stopped watching TV thirty years ago.

The influence of our culture has made witches and witchcraft appealing to today's teens. Growing up on Harry Potter books and movies has further opened doors for teens to experience both a curiosity and a familiarity with witchcraft. Increasingly, towns in the hub of America, once known for their strong Christian heritage, are becoming hotbeds for Wicca and Paganism.

The local town I live in currently is a hot spot as well. I was grocery shopping at Meijer's with my son, and a stranger saw the tattoo on the back of my neck. This tattoo is from my Wicca days and is very symbolic and telling. Lloyd has the same tattoo on his neck as well. This lady walked up to me and invited me to come and meet her NEWLY formed Coven in our small town.

I told her no thank you and explained that I now

follow a Christian belief. I prayed for this woman as we walked away. Young people are looking for power, and Wicca is a belief that promises supernatural power over their environment. Too often, they see Christians around them who are leading powerless lives. Films are also marketed and packaged very successfully to further those agendas.

Wicca uniquely appeals to women because it emphasizes the sacred feminine combined with a passion for caring for the earth and our environment. Women are highly valued, and even worshiped in most instances. The Wiccan *"religion"* is attracting men and women of all ages, and sadly Wicca is also known to be the fastest-growing religion in America. This frightens me to no end.

Modern Wiccans often present themselves and their beliefs as benevolent, stating that they don't worship Satan or sacrifice animals. They claim to be seeking to harness the earth's natural forces and use them for good. Guess what? This isn't always the case. Suppose there are no boundaries. Who is that gatekeeper? My bible is my boundary with my Christian faith; my Pastor, who I trust completely, is my boundary to the door of my church.

We need to teach our children that the Bible specifically condemns the practice of witchcraft and that practicing magic or spells is not just harmless fun. It is spoken about multiple times in the bible.

Deuteronomy 18:10

"Let no one be found among you who sacrifices their son or daughter in the fire, who practices divination or sorcery, interprets omens, engages in witchcraft."

Galatians 5:19-21

"The acts of the flesh are obvious: sexual immorality, impurity, and debauchery; idolatry and witchcraft; hatred, discord, jealousy, fits of rage, selfish ambition, dissensions, factions and envy; drunkenness, orgies, and the like. I warn you, as I did before, that those who live like this will not inherit the kingdom of God."

Even with all that I have stated, some of you still think, "It doesn't sound that bad." Just wait till I get into the parts about the ceremonial sacrificial rituals.

For you to fully understand my journey, I need to continue to tell you my personal story - the story of my journey from Darkness to Light. In the next chapter, we will be going a bit deeper into my personal story.

A couple of "choose to read" chapters at the end of the book will describe some 'truths' that people can't or refuse to imagine.

CHAPTER FOURTEEN
HISTORY REPEATS ITSELF

I got married young to an alcoholic who was sober for most of our relationship. This marriage blessed me with two bonus sons, Robert, and Jacob. They were about 3 and 5 when we got together. I was 21ish. He and I then had two children, Charles and Jarred. Jacob, my stepson, was a hyper and rambunctious little boy. While my other stepson Robert was a gentle old soul growing up, a caretaker of sorts, he was my big helper. Charles was our miracle baby; it took many rounds of infertility treatments to have our little boy. Jarred was a surprise to us after going thru what we did to get pregnant with Charles. Ultimately our little surprise ended up saving my life. They found Cancer when he was born, this caused me to have to undergo surgeries and treatments.

Looking back, I sometimes just shake my head. I was not the best mother then, but I did do the best I could. But I have learned to forgive myself and offer myself grace because I didn't know any different. I failed to provide the proper foundation for my children then. I hope they have forgiven me because I know I screwed up with my older children.

Looking back at this relationship, I created the foundation that I survived growing up. A family plagued with zero faith, with a lot of addiction and dysfunction.

I had my very own family dysfunctional family skit taking place. The difference is it was now in my own home.... AGAIN.

~Addict, check

~Enabler, check

~Mascot, check

~Hero, check

~The lost child, check

~The Scapegoat, check

Once again, the foundation that I allowed with my older children shaped and formed their life. There have been many challenges with them. Jacob died at the age of 19 and Jarred died at 18.

Robert and Charles have experienced more loss than any child I know. I will write more on this later.

We divorced in 2004 but have remained friends

throughout. It wasn't always easy, and I screwed up a lot. For what it is worth, I was pretty screwed up due to the Wicca, which I hid from my family. I believe my mother thought I left it long ago, and my ex-husband and children had no idea it was taking place, along with the dysfunction that was taking place in the home. I don't think that I breathed again until 2007.

Today, I am happily remarried to my high school sweetheart Myke. We got back together in 2007. Myke blessed me with two more bonus children, a boy named Gavin and a girl named Alexys. Myke and I now also have seven adopted children. I am thankful that we began our adoption journey together after finding our faith in Christ. We have tried hard to build a life from which we do not need a vacation from. We also make sure that our foundation is strong with Faith.

Our younger children have been brought up far differently than our older children. When I separate the "older from the younger" children, I want to be clear. Our younger children are those that we adopted from foster care. When I say far different, it's not even parallel. Finding my faith after such a dark road and losing Jacob and Jarred in the way we did has reshaped me as a parent. I'm so thankful for that today.

We began homeschooling with our first adopted son Oliver. In my opinion, it works better for our family. We don't utilize the public-school platform; I'm not saying that I don't support public schools, but we have decided to homeschool. We are raising children who already have trauma from their journey in foster care. We like choosing the content they learn and the ability to say, "No, we are not teaching that," if it doesn't align with our Christian belief.

We also don't allow any social media with the younger children. It is a gruesome world we live in, and the amount of knowledge that the internet can sift through our children's brains is frightening. Let's not even discuss the amount of grooming that takes place. But I will say this, if you as a parent are not willing to drop your child off in the middle of Disney world ALONE, don't leave them unsupervised on Social Media.

We have chosen to see our children's faces and not the top of their heads because they look down at the device. I'm not saying that if you allow your child to have social media, you're a terrible parent. If you allow your child to have social media, I am praying and hoping that you're having conversations with your child to keep them safe.

I work a lot with trafficked children, and almost ¾

of the children I work with met their trafficker on a social media platform. We have an agreement with our younger children regarding social media. We have discussed it A LOT. The deal is that once they are done with school and college, they can choose to have it if they want. I honestly think that given the number of discussions we have had and the fact that they have attended training's that I have done on the dangers of social media with our youth, none of them have the "want" for it. I think tech addiction is a real problem. In a real way, it destroys a child's brain. The tech addict dies slowly inside. Their personality changes, their mood changes, their brain changes, and their connection with family, friends, and the outside world all change.

Our younger children don't get a cell phone until they begin to drive for safety reasons. When they are home with their phone, there are rules, they stay on the main floor of the house, don't go into bedrooms or bathrooms, and we always know their passwords. They are OURS, not THEIRS. They have some privacy with them, but how we have raised them has given us trust in them.

I can hear some of you now, "How do they communicate with friends?" We still have a landline house phone that is wired into the wall for them to use to call friends. This phone costs us $20.00 a month; it's worth it. Not one of them complains about the limitations because, given the path that brought them into foster care, they prefer to know that we are trying to protect them from things they cannot control.

Proverbs 22:6

"Train up a child in the way he should go: and when he is old, he will not depart from it."

I broke the dysfunctional cycle in my home. It just took a little while for me to figure that out. There were a lot of excruciating lessons along the way, both in my life and my children's life. Sadly, sometimes even we parents must learn the hard way. But isn't that what we parents say to our children: "You will have to learn the hard way." Guess what, sometimes we do also.

I wish I had known what I know now in my marriages and being a parent. Sadly, I didn't, and a great price has been paid for it.

I am a testimony of someone who lost two children to the world, but I took it as a wake-up call and transformed my heart and efforts, resulting in saving the other children from the same fate. Even if you failed once, or in my case, twice, the promise is still accurate, and you can "Train up a child in the way he should go," knowing with a certainty, "He will not depart from it."

My story has a lot of broken pieces. I have failed multiple times in raising my children. In 2006, many things began to come to a head, but it wasn't until 2012, when Jacob passed, and I ultimately went dark, that I decided that I needed to do things differently. Even then, I didn't take the cues I was given.

These were pre-adopted children and pre-faith. In writing this book, it was hard. I wanted to share some bad and equally share some of the good. In doing so, it might jump around a bit. The next chapter will deal specifically with my Demise of witchcraft.

CHAPTER FIFTEEN
THE PARTIAL DEMISE OF TRINITY AND WICCA

The word "Partial" is interesting because it means limited, incomplete, restricted, imperfect, and unfinished. That completely sum's up this whole chapter. I began to start to question some things revolving around Wicca in 2006. During this time, things began to turn a bit sour.

> **"The more I learned, the more things started to spiral downward, deeper and deeper into darkness and black magic."**

I had become good at what I was practicing. Although Natas never acknowledged Satan, he said there was something called 'the abyss' that we should avoid. Remember that red flag I wrote about earlier that was bigger than the Atlantic Ocean? Insert red flag there...

It was late 2006 when I began to question a lot of the things I had been taught and many of the things I had ventured and learned on my own. I won't say I quit practicing because that would be an absolute lie. But I did begin to question everything my own life included. I believe that I was on the path of my redemption.

I was still not one hundred percent willing to dismiss it entirely, but I was trying to find my way. This was a difficult journey, but a journey I was learning to navigate.

During this time, I did pack my spell book, alter ritual supplies, and everything that revolved around Wicca in a large tote and placed it in an area of my house that was off-limits. I did not understand my intention in packing things away this way. However, I did feel it was the right thing to do at this point. I just had this feeling that there was so much more for me out there.

It was a very interesting time in that I wasn't explicitly practicing Wicca, and I certainly wasn't following a path of Christianity either. I was just sitting in the middle of doing nothing about anything spiritually. I am not sure if this was for the better or, the worse.

This went on for years, in fact, almost seven. I sat in what I would call a parallel universe, unsure of what was right and wrong.

I feel like I was beginning to make some headway in figuring out my screwed-up, skewed reality of faith. I remember living in a small house on the lake; I would wake up, walk to the sliding glass door in my bedroom, look out at the lake first thing in the morning, and think to myself, "What the hell should I do now?"

I knew two things. One, Wicca could no longer rule my life, and Two, that I needed to get my shit together fast because what I was doing was no longer working for me.

In 2007 when Myke and I got back together, he never really knew much about my past from when he and I split up when we were younger until twelvish years later when we got back together. I often wonder if there would be an us today had he known it all. He does know it all now, and he and I are still happily married. He, at that time, just knew I wasn't into any form of religion and was a non-believer in Christ. He did know that there was a dark side to my past, but he never really questioned anything about it.

Without any certainty, I can say that I did not practice magic on a daily or even in ritual format since 2007. In fact, during this time, I only had contact with Lloyd and Christine. The rest of my

Coven had gone separate ways into their covens. I was just sitting in the parallel of the unsure.

Until 2012.........

When everything went completely DARK.

CHAPTER SIXTEEN
THE EXTIRPATION UNFOLDING

Jacob lived in his hometown with a friend and his mother, and he had some struggles. Jacob and I did remain in contact after his father, and I divorced. He would often come and fish with my husband, go to wrestling meets to root on his brothers, and visit when he could. He loved animals; in fact, he had a ton of them. He was a child that would let a bug outside because he did not want to harm it.

One day, Jacob was about 15, and we were camping at a local campground. A huge water snake came into the beach area. All the girls, myself included, began screaming and running out of the water. To us, it was more like an anaconda than a small water snake. Jacob walked into the water, grabbed the snake, put it into a bucket, and decided to relocate it to the front lake where people did not swim. I would have just killed the snake. Ok.... I would have just had my husband kill the snake, but Jacob went out of his way to preserve it and relocate it.

He walked with his little brother's bucket in hand with a towel over it to the front lake, which was quite a long walk. He went onto the dock and started to release the snake, only to realize that it was no longer in the bucket. They backtracked and found it near a volleyball court at the campground. He put it back into the bucket again, put the towel over the snake, and tried again. He put the snake back into its natural habitat without harming it. Most people would not have put that much effort into releasing a snake and just let it be wherever it was.

Jacob was more concerned with the children playing at the nearby park and volleyball court. He cared more about the safety of the children playing and the snake than the amount of time it took him to backtrack.

Jacob had a love for life and everyone in it. He was a stellar 6' 4 inch, 180-pound man. I could put both of my feet inside one of his shoes. He was an athlete who loved to wrestle at his high school. He was obsessed with reptiles and exotic animals. I believe he wanted to pursue something in that line of work one day, perhaps working at a zoo.

Early April 2012, I received a call from Jacob. He was 19 years old at the time. He called and said he wanted to come home from where he was living for Easter and celebrate his 20th birthday that year. His little brothers and I were ecstatic because the last time he was home was a few months prior. Sometimes when our children become adults, they often don't choose to come home. So, I always really appreciated it when they did.

We planned the days and things he wanted to do. He mainly wanted to hang out with his little brothers and fish some with Myke. We discussed his menu choices of what he would like to eat while home. This always made me laugh because he always picked the same thing. I could count on his options each time, but I still asked.

We chit-chatted for a bit more about different things. I remember giving him some grief over his taste in music like I always had. Jacob LOVED heavy metal; the heavier, the better. *Asking Alexandria* was his favorite. This day, I could hear a song by his favorite band playing in the background on the phone. I jokingly said, "Son, that music is terrible," he responded, "It's my lullaby." I had to laugh when he said this because even as a child, he loved music.

During this call, he said he had been going thru some struggles of his own with addiction and some mental health issues. It broke my heart hearing some of the struggles he was having. I didn't want to push too much during this call, and I decided to wait until he got here to finish this conversation. I just let him talk as I listened.

While I was on the phone with him, I remember having a gut feeling that something was off, but I could not quite put my finger on it. How often do we second guess our gut instincts when involving our adult children as a mother? I did this day when speaking with Jacob. Would this of changed his mind about coming home a day later? Likely not. But maybe had I had just a bit more time with him on the phone, I would have learned more about what was happening with him.

Often as parents of adult children, we take a back seat to whatever they seem to have going on in their lives at the time. I wish I had been more intentional during this call. I was just excited for him to come home and spend Easter and his birthday with us at my mom's house. He was so tall that he could hide the Easter eggs up high, and the kids had to climb on his shoulders to find them.

So as a mother, in my mind, I just went on planning the week with him. I did not ask many questions, and I just wanted him to come spend some time with us. He asked me if he could call me right back; he had another call he had to take. I said yes, half expecting him to forget to call me back as our kids do.

I remember getting off the phone and looking at Myke and saying, "Jacob is coming, but something isn't right." Myke brushed it off, not thinking any different. I called his older brother Robert and let him know Jacob was coming to visit, letting him know he was welcome to come hang out with us as well.

About 10 minutes later, Jacob called me back. I am not sure what transpired in that call; I did not ask for details. Jacob told me that he would be coming home a day later than we originally planned because he would be with his friend. I did not want to argue about it. I knew he had been going thru a lot of stuff and I just wanted to see him. I told him that was fine and to be careful. He said he would, and then we hung up. I sent him a text message immediately after saying, "Not feeling good about this," he responded, "I'll be fine; don't worry about me, see you in a couple of days." I replied, "Love you," and he responded, "Love you too."

I am encouraged that the words we shared were based on love. I got to tell him I loved him, and he got to say he loved me as well. We had a great conversation that day and shared a lot of laughs.

Although I know Jacob knew that I loved him, a part of me knows that I could have told him more. Can a child be told that they are loved too much? I certainly don't believe that is true.

Today I am incredibly thankful that I got to tell Jacob I loved him. I didn't know that this would be the last time I would have the opportunity to speak with him.

I am 100% sure that when Jacob went to his eternity, he knew that he was loved. I do take comfort in this. You never really know when the last conversation will occur; it is a blessing and a curse.

The following day Jacob was a victim of a double murder-suicide when an ex-boyfriend of his friend broke into the home and killed him, his friends' mother, and then killed himself. My stepson died from blunt force trauma to the head with an ax.

In a matter of an instant, five families were destroyed. Mine, his father's, his mother's, the perpetrators', and the surviving friend's family.

I remember the day, time, weather outside, what was cooking on the stove, and what I was doing when I felt my world crashing down.

My boys were at their fathers for an extended weekend. That day they were at a local amusement-type park. It was raining outside but just starting to clear up. Myke was in the shed putting some things up.

I remember opening the sliding door to smell the rain. Alexys asked, "What are you doing?" and I stated, "I love the smell right after a good rain."

It was early afternoon when Alexys handed me the phone that was ringing. I was cooking at the time. I remember looking down at the caller ID and thinking to myself. "Great, one of the boys must be sick." I answered the phone "Hey," knowing it was their father. I heard a pause, then one word, "ANG" it was not just "Ang"; it was more like "AANNNNNGGGGGG." It was strangled, urgent, and heartbreaking. I had never heard his voice in this tone before. I think my heart may have stopped for a moment. I immediately said, "What happened?" and I looked at Alexys and said, "Go get your dad, please," as he was still in the shed. I knew something was wrong just by the tone of his voice. I then walked into my room and shut the door. I said, "What's wrong? What happened? Are the boys, okay?"

I did not know what it was; I just knew it wasn't good. I heard him take a deep inhaled breath, but

I do not remember him ever exhaling aloud. To this day, I can still hear this in my mind; it was as if he had forgotten how to breathe. The following words from his mouth still haunt me today in my sleep. "ANG, I don't know.... O MY GOD.... I can't.... O MY GOD...This cannot be real." I got upset and yelled at him, "What happened?" "Where are the boys?" He replied, "Jacob is dead. O, MY GOD, Jacob was killed, I don't know all the details yet, but Jacob is dead." I immediately dropped to my knees. After hearing a bit of the conversation, my husband walked into our bedroom and attempted to comfort me, and I lashed out. I was mean and hateful. I was just awful.

Things went into a blur; anger set in, disbelief, fear - a strong distaste for God, who I did not even believe in. I needed someone else to blame.

Within a few months before Jakes's passing, I had begun to seriously question many things revolved around Wicca. Also, my sense of belonging within that practice, but I still did not believe there was another way. I certainly was not looking to make a "faith" change soon. I had just begun to question the "moral compass" of things that I knew regarding it.

That is so difficult for me to say today. I blamed a God that I did not even believe in taking my child away. I did not blame the act of free will of the person who killed him. It was easier to blame someone I did not believe in than blame the mental health and free will of those who killed him. I had nothing better to do at that time because I had quit living myself.

I began going thru the motions. The motions of getting lost in myself, in my pity and grief. Thru this process of desperation, I lost myself, but I also became a shell of who I should have been and a person I do not even know. I began failing at being a mother, became a distant wife, and sadly I just felt like I died along with Jacob. Honestly, a part of me did die for an exceptionally long time. Every day was just "motions"; there was no substance to any of it. Get up, put boys on the bus, go back to bed, get boys off the bus, make dinner, eat, put boys to bed, stay up reading all night, and do it all over.

Remember me saying earlier; that some things did not seem right when I spoke with Jacob. There was more I did not know but was finding out thru media outlets.

The media did not understand that this was my child, my children's brother, mother's grandchild, brother's nephew, niece, and nephew's cousin, not their "news" he had a family, young siblings, and friends. We had not even had a chance to tell our family what they were releasing about my child. This added so much grief to the situation that was already unbearable. Then there are the news outlets that spread lies for clicks and likes.

My children never got the chance to grieve their brother. I never got the opportunity to grieve my son. I think I slept for the first year of it and read. My mind remained in a very dark place for a very long time.

I am not saying this was a healthy way to deal with my grief, but it worked for what I needed at that time. So, I began to sleep, eat, read, and do it all over again. In the end, I gained almost 100 pounds. I went from a size 14 to a 26 of pure miserable anger and dysfunction.

Did I mention I still had zero faith? I still blamed God for losing my son. Part of me blamed myself for things I did in my past. That Three-fold Law did encompass my mind a few times or more like a million times. I began having nightmares of things that I had previously done in Wicca. This didn't help my already neglected sleeping routine.

I self-destructed right before my husband's eyes. I lost so much time with my other children and my husband in doing so. How ironic is this? I lost Jacob, which destroyed my world as I knew it, only to allow that to take me away from my other children and husband. They were alive and well and needed a mother and wife to support and take care of them.

I look back on this now, and I can say. "Man, I SERIOUSLY MESSED UP." My husband, Myke, is my best friend and my rock, and he did the best he could to keep up with everything. The fact that he did not leave me during this time still amazes me.

I can only imagine how fun it was to live within our walls during that time. Even as I sit here and type this, I get tears in my eyes because of what I put my family through, he not only had to be a father to our four young children, but he had to be a mother as well.

My children were angry and acting out. I failed to see any of it because I isolated myself to the point that I became a prisoner in my mind. My children, in essence, learned to live without their mother because I was nonexistent and unavailable to their needs. So, I allowed them to lose their mother, who was alive and well-ish, AFTER just losing their brother.

Also, there was a trail of death from 2009 on to make matters worse. We lost my father's lifetime best friend Lee, my paternal grandparents

Charles and Dorothy in May of 2009; then, within six weeks, we lost my father on June 13, 2009. This all took place within six weeks. The level of Grief that just stacked upon itself was all earth-shattering. It was like layer upon layer of pure sadness, anger, and defeat.

People from the outside looking in thought everything was ok, in fact, I heard daily, "You're the strongest person I know." No. I was not. I was failing miserably, and my children were lost amid the chaos in my mind.

My children and I had never properly healed from the loss of my father and other family members, then got a huge blow when Jacob died. I just thought that "God" liked taking people I loved because of stuff I had done in the past. That is no excuse, my children and husband needed me, and I could not even be there because I was consumed with things in a non-biblical and unhealthy way.

Looking back, I am in awe of the grace and favor that God showed me during this time. I did not even understand it, and I did NOT deserve it. But he gave it to me without me even knowing because I still did not believe in him.

We were part of a local campground, the same one that Jacob went to with us when he saved the beach from the anaconda snake that wanted to eat everyone alive.

Ironically, it was a Christian-based campground. We liked it because it was safe and secure for the kids to roam freely. It is incredible how God placed people in our lives that He knew we needed.

Again, proving to me He had the plan already made for us all along. He placed us in the very place that my family needed when we needed it. Looking back now at the events surrounding how we came to know this camp and the people there, there is only one answer. This was God's divine intervention in that I began to allow God to step in and change the outcome of the situation that was actively destroying me. Spending summers at this campground with my family began to change my foundation that was broken.

To be completely transparent on this, I still struggle today with **ONE FACT**, the **ONE FACT** that I helped cause in Jacob's foundation, the **ONE FACT** that I never personally had the conversation with him about, the **ONE FACT** that still haunts me in my sleep on some nights.

"I DO NOT KNOW IF JACOB WAS A BELIEVER IN CHRIST AND ACCEPTED HIM INTO HIS HEART."

This **ONE FACT** is my fault, and I take full responsibility. Because of this, I cannot attest to where his eternity lays. You heard me right. Today, I am hopeful that he was much brighter than I was at that time in his life. I am optimistic that he knew then what I know now. This is something I will not know the answer to until I am brought home to my eternity.

CHAPTER SEVENTEEN
THE AWAKENING OF FAITH

My personal story is filled with shattered pieces, questionable choices, and some gruesome truths. I have done some very dark things in my life. But that same story is also filled with MAJOR comebacks and a rebirth. Guess what; yours is also! Not one of us reading this can say that we have lived without mistakes.

My testimony of faith is not what one would think of as normal if there is such a thing. Coming from a position of the "Wicked Witch of the West," to a place in "Christianity," came with its struggles internally and spiritually.

Later, ok, much later. I finally took the plunge in faith. I had been invited to a local church by a lady named Jessica, but I did not go. I stayed noticeably clear of anything to do with it - lying to her and explaining why I could not attend. What was I going to say to her, "I can't go because the church might just burn down or implode if I enter?" As I said, I had been questioning the "Practice of Wicca" for a while now. But I was not quite ready to try something else yet. Because let's face it, my faith was working so well for me, right? So, I lied to her, "I can't come because I can't bring my kids." She gracefully smiled at me and said "okay." I went on about my business and didn't think about it again, Until...

On a different day, I went into the same local establishment with my then younger children and was invited to church again by Jessica. But this time, she began by telling me about the children's programs they had, thinking that my kids would enjoy them.

She told me this while I was in line to get snacks with my children. My son looked at me and said, "Let's go, Mom; that sounds fun." I thought to myself, "Well played, Jessica, I just wanted a darn hot pretzel with cheese sauce." I agreed to try it out sometime. I didn't say when.

I still did not go; it took a couple of months for me to pull my head from my rear end. I knew my husband would be resistant to a new change. But one night, while sleeping, I had a dream of us all being in church together. I still did not go; the following week was a trying week with appointments and court hearings. I may have had a root canal scheduled, a pedicure, a haircut, and multiple other "stupid excuses."

Because, let's face it, I didn't make it a priority even after having the dream of all of us attending church together. I continued to make excuse after excuse as to why I could not, should not, and wouldn't attend. Again, they were nothing but excuses because you make time for what's important.

I had to make a conscious effort to decide to take responsibility or continue making excuses for the foundation that I was allowing with my family.

To take responsibility, I had to take ownership and the initiative to make this change in our home. This would be a considerable change, in fact, opposite to what they knew. I was expecting some resistance. But I just decided this was going to happen.

That following Sunday, I woke up and decided we were going. I packed up our younger children and did just that; we went. I am talking no planning, no warning to any of them, no setting out church clothing. Nope. I just woke up and said, "Get dressed; we are going to church." None of the children had a complaint or issue with getting up early on a Sunday, getting dressed, and out the door by a specific time.

I was half geared up for a meltdown or two from one of my children. I was pleasantly surprised.

They were dressed and out the door in record time.

As we took the 10-minute drive to where we were going, I reminded them of all the things my grandparents had told me when we were heading to church. Behave, Sit still, etc. I must have heard "OKAY MOM" ten times during that drive. I remember pulling into the parking lot and letting out a big sigh. Was I about to do this?

I sat in my van with my children, bouncing in their seats with anticipation of walking inside.

Little did they know I was contemplating turning my van around and driving back home. The thoughts running thru my mind at that time were telling me that I was not worthy enough to be accepted into a fellowship of Faith. Oh, and perhaps a little of "What If I ignite and catch fire in front of their eyes." I looked into the rearview mirror, and my son looked at me and said, "Are we gonna sit here all day or what?" I made a quick calculation noting that the fire department was less than three blocks away, just if this "Witch" caught fire walking into a Christian faith Church. We got out and made our way to my new "Faith and Home" doors.

Once we started attending church services we made significant changes in our home. We began being Christ-centered. I slowly began finding my voice again. I began to read and try to understand the bible. I started to find scripture that could directly tell me I was going to hell if I continued down the prior dark path again.

Because I still was tempted all the time with the "Dark Side." I remember one morning waking up, and my young son's brown leather bible that had a tree on the cover was sitting on the kitchen table. Pastor Rob gifted him this bible at camp; he carried it everywhere. It was sitting on my kitchen table and was lying open. A little yellow party napkin was lying on a page, and it was underlining a verse perfectly. It made no sense to me at the time. Where did the yellow party napkin even come from? How did it underline perfectly the verse Micah 5:12?

Micah 5:12

"I will destroy your witchcraft and you will no longer cast spells."

To this day, I have no idea how that happened. I had not been reading the bible. It was not even in that same room. Our younger children were with my husband at camp. He was giving me a break to get a few needed things done in the house. This is still a complete mystery to me, perhaps God's divine intervention? But when something blatantly comes and slaps you in the face, you obey. I sat at our kitchen table and read that verse multiple times. I wondered how this bible was opened to Micah, with that yellow napkin underling the very verse I needed to see, read, and then read again.

I then decided to go further and search for more. I opened my phone and searched the words "bible scripture on witchcraft and evil," making a note of a few. I was shocked to see there were nearly 100 biblical scriptures regarding Witchcraft. It hit me like a ton of bricks as I sat there reading some scripture in my son's little brown bible with the imprinted tree on the front telling me everything I wish I had known when I was 16 years old.

That day it ended. I took my small black hardcover book that contained almost 20 years of Wicca writings, spells, rituals, effects, and the journal of my practices, along with everything that had anything to do with the "dark side," walked outside, put it in the small fireplace burn pit we had in the corner of our yard and burned it all. I sat there and watched what was happening in that small burn pit. I watched almost 20 years of my life burn, and I did not have one uneasy feeling or concern about this. It gave me a sense of calmness, freedom, positivity, and complete peace for the first time in a long time. The more I surrendered myself to Jesus; the more my family life began to fall into place. The more I started understanding the words in the bible, the more I healed. The difference became words jumping off the pages at me versus not understanding a word I read before that day.

It was not until Jesus Christ completely wiped me clean and rebuilt me that I could process the thought of Grief and missing my child. Let me repeat this:

IT WASN'T UNTIL I SURRENDERED, SURRENDERED IT ALL TO JESUS CHRIST, AND LET HIM REBUILD ME, LEVEL ME, AND HEAL ME THAT I BEGAN ACTUALLY TO LIVE AGAIN.

I completely surrendered my life and accepted my Savior Jesus Christ on September 18th, 2018, at the same lake that my son Jacob saved us from the anaconda snake many years prior.

I know that I have so much farther to go in my relationship with Christ. But I know I can do all things thru Him because He genuinely does strengthen me. But I cannot ever lose my faith again because He is not done with me yet.

Once I saw what Christ could do in my "broken"

home, it became a non-negotiable rule in the house. I had already screwed up with my now-adult children by not prioritizing this. I failed them in this, just as my parents unintentionally failed me.

I continued to go and get involved with our church. The more involved I became, the more I noticed my younger children asking to partake. It was a great transition in every way, shape, and form. Every Saturday, my children began asking, "Do we get to go to church tomorrow?" They enjoyed it and looked forward to it. We became a family of faith.

What an epiphany.

Let me tell you this, and this is just my perspective. I am not raising our kids in the church so they can grow up perfect. I'm not raising our kids in the church because it magically makes them unable to sin or holier-than-thou.

However, I am raising our kids in the church so they know just who to run to when they mess up and when they fall. So, they know that he will never leave them, no matter how big or small their mess up might be. So they will understand what grace is like and give it out freely. So, they will know the unconditional love and love of those around them, regardless of anything else. So, they know that there is absolutely nothing in this world they could do that His blood hasn't already atoned for.

I will never apologize for raising my younger children in church. I will never apologize for making sure our family prioritizes the church over anything else because it's more than just a song and a sermon. It's more than just a memorized bible verse in class. It's for when this cruel world we live in comes knocking on their door. They know the solid rock on which they stand.

It's so they know they are not too dirty, that He can't cleanse. It's so they know they will never be too guilty for God to love and forgive. It's so they know they will never be so far gone that God cannot reach. It's so they will see that they are not too broken for God to fix no matter what.

I will continue to apologize for not raising my now-adult children as Christians. I have learned the hard way. The upbringing that I had, combined with the untruths of religion I was taught at a young age, was my reason for that. However, it was my responsibility to fix myself so that I could give them a better foundation.

CHAPTER EIGHTEEN
PAINFULLY BROKEN

We had Christmas 2017 at my Mom's that year; we were there as a family. We did the traditional things, opened gifts, ate a traditional supper, and spent time together. Jarred's friend was picking him back up at about 8:30 PM. I made all my kids stand for a family photo, not knowing that would be the last picture that we took of Jarred. I remember Charles griping about having to take a picture. Like he always did, because he hates pictures. I even said, "Hey, what if it is the last one?" as I put my kids in line, the adult children in the back and the younger children in front and snapped the button on my phone.

I remember thinking to myself that something was not right. But with Jarred, it was different because with him, you just never knew, there was always something not right, but you picked your battles. He was standing, alive, not in handcuffs, and was present. Mothers who have dealt with children in trouble will understand that mother's instinct and the dismissal that something was not right. I took a few more pictures with my phone, and we all said our goodbyes.

I hugged Jarred tight and whispered in his ear. "Be careful, son; I love you." He replied, "I love you too, don't worry about me. I'll be fine," as he walked out the door. That rang in my head because Jarred did not even know that is almost verbatim what Jacob said to me the last time I spoke to him.

I still have issues today with people who do not say "Bye," it triggers me in a way that is still not entirely healthy. I am talking about when I am speaking to someone on the phone and they hang up without saying goodbye. I will call them back to find out if their phone is broken, if they died, or hung up on me.

We left my mom's that night and headed home exhausted. I had texted Jarred a "goodnight" at about 10:10 PM. I did not get a text back, but this was not unusual because his phone battery was always dead, or he would often respond much later. Being a snarky mom, I sent a second text, "If you don't start responding to my texts, I'm going to think you're dead, or I may just shut your phone off." Again, I got nothing back, which was not abnormal, he would respond later, and I would wake up to the text, or so I thought. So, my husband and I crawled into bed exhausted and fell asleep. I remember praying that night to God, thanking him for such a great day at my mom's house and the opportunity to see my kids all together. I asked Him to keep them all safe and for His will to be done.

I was awakened by my phone in the early hours of the morning to one word, the one word that had haunted me in my sleep since 2012. The very word I heard in early April 2012. I looked at the caller ID, knowing my Ex did not have any of the boys this time. I knew something was terribly wrong. He had no reason to call me that early. I got out of bed, already in a panic, pacing in our bedroom. I answered this time, "Hello," and I heard the very word that rocked my world in 2012. "AAANNNNGGGGG," even more strangled than the last time.

I dropped to the floor because I knew it was about Jarred by the process of elimination. Alexys and Charles came back here to stay with their younger siblings after leaving my mom's; Gavin was at his house, and Robert was at his home with his wife and two sons. I KNEW it was about Jarred. I began screaming, "NO NO NO!" My husband woke up in a panic, wondering what was wrong. Jarred's dad said, "O my God, not again. AAANNNNGGG, I don't even know how to say this. I can't even say it;

Jarred is dead, it was an accident, but he is dead." I dropped to the ground. I did not say a word. He went on, "He was shot, it was an accident, he shot himself in the head, but they said it was an accident." I do not remember what I said next. Everything came back to me; it was a blur.

I sent Myke downstairs to wake up the older kids and gave him a verbal list of calls to make. I remember saying to him precisely as he walked out of the door and headed downstairs. "Do not call my mom; I will call her. Do not call my mom. She has to hear this from me."

He walked out of the room, phone in hand, in shock, I am sure. I dropped to my knees sobbing, and I prayed,

"God, I can't do this again without You; please surround me with Your peace and show me what I need to do this time. This is going to be hard for everyone; he was a huge part of people's lives. Do not let me screw up this time. Help me to not go down that Wide path again, keep me on Your Narrow road; God help me get through this, knowing he is now home with You. Amen."

I still remember that prayer like it was yesterday. I picked up the phone and called my mom, and she answered on the first ring. I swear she never sleeps. I said, "Hello, Mom," she replied, "What happened, is it Jarred?" I replied simply, "I need you to come now." She replied, "Ok, I'm on my way." She didn't even say "Bye." She just hung up.

After we hung up, I sat on my bed for a few moments before going downstairs. I remember looking up and saying aloud, **"No, I can't do this again, GOD I CANNOT do this again."** It was clear as day. I heard it; I listened to the Holy Spirit speak to me,

> *"Do good, do good deeds, reach people, help people, turn every hurt into grace and good, stay in the light, use his story, and help as many people as he would have."*

I stood up and felt this overwhelming peace enter my body. I took a deep breath, feeling my lungs inflate with oxygen. It was bizarre but in a beautiful way. I opened the door to our bedroom and stopped at the landing that led to the downstairs. As I sat in a paused state and listened to our daughter Alexys cry, I knew I had a choice to make, be obedient or self-destruct.

I walked downstairs with my head held high into the living room where the older kids were sitting. Charles, I believe, was in shock, and Alexys was sobbing. I began to see the destruction that would soon occur all over again. The scene played out like a "lifetime movie" in front of me.

I looked around and made a choice. I remember looking up and nodding to the ceiling, and I decided then and there, and I went into action in memory of my son Jarred.

I would take every hurt feeling of grief I had and turn it into something good. I was going to touch people with his story and reach as many people as possible. I would obey the Holy Spirit and do exactly as instructed.

I remember when my mom walked into the house with Terry. I heard her ask my husband, "How is she?" He replied, "She is ok." My mother said, "She is in shock; she is not okay." Nope, I was entirely at peace. I was not in shock at all; I had a new purpose in my life. I was honoring the memory of my son in a way that was healthy and to help as many people as possible. The main difference is that I chose to HONOR my son's memory, but I decided to HONOR Christ first.

I had peace knowing that Jarred was in his eternal home with Christ, because I showed Jarred who Christ was before he passed away. Jarred was about 17 when he went to church with us, and just a few days before his death, he served our church

Communion. I know he knew Christ when he had his homecoming. Did I hurt? Yes. Was I mad? Yes. Was this going to define me this time? NO. My foundation had changed, and in changing that, my face of grief changed. I was now experiencing something surreal, and to be quite honest, it was beautiful.

The day was a blur; most of my family knew as they were enroute when my mother made it to the house. I made it an intentional decision to deliver the news personally to each of his close friends. I did just that to every single friend that walked in my door. "Have a seat; I need to talk to you; he's gone, Jarred is gone." I can still close my eyes and see the faces of each person I told this to.

For me, taking something "bad" and using it to give "good" was how I lived through the loss of Jarred. When most people lose one child, it cripples them; I know because it did me. But to have the opportunity to have a 'Do-Over', as I did, I could not do the same thing I did before. I did not want to become the true definition of pure insanity again.

With Jacob, I had zero faith; in fact, I was destructive and on a path back to the dark side. With Jarred, I can say that my faith was bigger than my grief. I could have fallen back into old habits of questionable Magic and destruction. But I didn't because I was obedient to the instructions I was given at one of the most vulnerable moments in my life.

We often treat our sins this way; we know that something is sinful, yet we resolve to "improve our behavior later." Or we only want to obey God when it's convenient for us. That's Satan's lie, "Enjoy this today; you can always obey tomorrow when it's more convenient...just have a little pleasure now. You can improve your behavior tomorrow." Delayed obedience is NOT obedience. Whatever obedience you are delaying, put your sin to death and obey God today!

CHAPTER NINETEEN
MOTIVATIONS FOR SERVING GOD

Why do we as Christians serve God? Why should we serve God? Many have probably never paused to consider their motives. While we do not need to understand our motives to serve God, or to grow in godliness, the more we are aware of them, the better we will be able to serve God as He deserves.

There are multiple things that should motivate us to serve God. But the one mighty thing is:

LOVE

The best way to get motivated to serve God is to love God. If we love God, it makes us automatically love others a bit more because God is love, but God is also a disciplinarian.

1 John 4:8

"Whoever does not love does not know God because God is love."

John 3:16

"For God so loved the world, that He gave His only begotten Son, that whosoever believeth in Him should not perish, but have everlasting life."

Without love, we lose the whole purpose. After all, God loves us. We need to be His hands and feet and serve others to serve God. Early in my faith journey, I was the type of Christian who went to church on Sundays to ask for all my sins to be forgiven so that on Monday morning, I was clean and could start over.

I had the wrong motivation for serving God. More of a convenience. Looking back today, I am still in Awe of the grace He gave me when I didn't deserve it.

To properly serve God, I had to make an intentional effort to love and serve Him actively. I still fail daily, but this is an area of growth that will be constant.

To love and serve God, you must:

1. Fall in love with God, and instead of asking Him for anything, just spend some time worshipping Him and thanking Him. List everything He has done for you, and just seek a relationship with Him.

2. Pray the scripture of Psalm 139:23-24. Ask God to clear your heart of any intentions that aren't reflective of Him to redirect your path.

Psalms 139:23-24

"Search me, God, and know my heart; test me and know my anxious thoughts. See if there is any offensive way in me and lead me in the way everlasting."

3. Listen for His Answers; listen to God's answers for your life. Pray before you read the Bible to invite God to speak to you in new ways.

4. Always turn back to Him, all day, every day.

There are so many more legitimate biblical motivations to follow and serve God but be warned; there are just as many illegitimate ones. We should learn to seek the highest motivations in our service. We should also learn to motivate others toward service or godliness with the best motivations. It is healthy to evaluate our motives for serving God and for growing in godliness so that we might serve Him better.

The Bible presents some powerful and clear motivations for godly living. Good motives may overlap, and some seem higher in theory than others.

In my opinion, I have learned that there are actually six easily recognizable motives for godly living. I already discussed Love a bit previously, but I will add it here again.

1. **Love:** This includes first love for God, then an accompanying love for others.

2. **Gratitude:** We may wish to respond gratefully because we benefit from God's actions. Our service and our lives become a "Thank You" to Him.

3. **Eternal Significance:** According to God's original purposes, we can be motivated to fulfill our longing for some significance beyond this temporary life. God created us to participate in His rule over us.

4. **Rewards:** We can also be motivated by God-given rewards in this life.

5. **Duty:** Some Christians will serve God because they have committed to do so or live up to what God has called them to do. Duty does not expect a reward but is performed out of obligation.

6. **Fear:** This motivation is inferior to love but can motivate the Christian away from sin or unfaithfulness and towards godly conduct.

> One might fear a negative judgment at the judgment seat of Christ, which can include shame or loss of reward. The Christian may also fear God's temporal discipline.

I know number six-well; God has disciplined me multiple times. Because we are His children, God does choose to discipline us. He does so in several ways. I have personally experienced the discipline of God, and I hope that everyone else has experienced it as well.

The issue is not how He disciplines us but the Why. The answer is simple, to conform us to the image of His Son. It is like chipping away everything in our lives that is not like Christ. It is a painful process, but the more shapeless stone we have, the more chipping is required. The more chipping, the more pain, for unlike stone, we feel, we hurt, and we question.

Is this part of God's discipline?

If you are currently undergoing the Lord's "spanking," focus on what He is trying to do in your life more than getting out of the "spanking."

You can break your knees in prayer, but if it is not God's will, it won't happen. When you pray, God listens; when you listen, God speaks; when you believe, miracles can happen.

I strive now never to forget that I still need God on my best days just as desperately as I do on my worst days. This includes times that He disciplines me. I want to hear the words "Well done," when I have my final homecoming.

CHAPTER TWENTY
BEAUTIFULLY REDEEMED

The starting point of being where God wants you to be, and doing the things God wants you to do, is surrendering your life completely, and unconditionally to Him. It is the only thing that God has ever asked us to do. The Bible says that if you have accepted Christ as your Savior, it is no longer your life; it belongs to Him.

We were never meant to fulfill, sort out and fix things on our own because the transformation we need most requires wisdom and power far beyond ours. This is why Paul wrote,

2 Thessalonians 1:11-12

"So, we keep on praying for you, asking our God to enable you to live a life worthy of His call. May He give you the power to accomplish all the good things your faith prompts you to do. Then the name of our Lord Jesus will be honored because of the way you live, and you will be honored along with Him. This is all made possible because of the grace of our God and Lord, Jesus Christ."

Everything is for the good of God's kingdom, which is the only kind we should pursue, whether it's weight loss, spiritual discipline, a potential marriage partner, or anything else. Every work of faith requires the power and wisdom of God because the outcomes God wants are more significant than we can produce.

God set it up this way to experience the highest, multilayered, fruit-producing joy from each outcome, and so His multifaceted glory would shine most brightly through us. If we understand this from the start, we can receive as God's gift the joyous feeling we experience when we first decide to carry out a work of faith. God grants us a preview of future grace and helps us get started. But it is not a balloon to float us over the rugged road. God wants far more for us than we typically want for ourselves.

I am blessed that I was spared. God saw more in me than I saw in myself at that time. With some of the things that I did, taught, and summoned upon myself and others. I could have quickly been pushed down a different path: that good old Wide path and Narrow Road. I took the Wide path for most of my life. I sit here on the Narrow road today as a survivor and redeemed.

When we speak of something or someone being

"redeemed," that implies there was originally a defect or shortcoming that is somehow made up for through redemption. To use a simplified example, a sports team might "redeem" their losing streak by winning in the final, most important game.

In the case of Christian redemption, we must first define what that defect or shortcoming is which needs to be redeemed. This passage in Romans is an excellent explanation of redemption through Christ:

Romans 3:23-26

"For everyone has sinned; we all fall short of God's glorious standard. Yet God, in His grace, freely makes us right in His sight. He did this through Christ Jesus when He freed us from the penalty for our sins. For God presented Jesus as the sacrifice for sin. People are made right with God when they believe that Jesus sacrificed His life, shedding His blood. This sacrifice shows that God was being fair when He held back and did not punish those who sinned in times past, for He was looking ahead and including them in what He would do in this present time. God did this to demonstrate His righteousness, for He himself is fair and just, and He makes sinners right in His sight when they believe in Jesus."

The sin of humankind is the flaw or defect that needs to be redeemed. Regardless of whether they believe in God, every person naturally has a sinful state. This sin separates us from God. The bible tells us that the penalty for sin is death - spiritual death, eternal separation from God.

The sin of humankind is the flaw or defect that needs to be redeemed. Regardless of whether they believe in God, every person naturally has a sinful state.

Unlike a losing sports team, WE can't redeem ourselves. We could never pay the penalty for our sins on our own, and there is no way we could ever do anything "good enough" to earn our way into redemption. This is where Jesus comes in!

When I finally pulled my head out of my rear end and believed in Christ, He "redeemed" or "purchased" me "through His blood." This word for "redeemed" is significant. At the time of the writing of the New Testament, it meant to go to the marketplace and buy an enslaved person who was in trouble and then set the enslaved person free. This is what Jesus did for us when He shed "His blood" on the cross. He came to the marketplace where we have been slaves to sin and He paid the price or ransom for all our sins with "His blood" and set us free.

I WAS ENSLAVED TO MY SIN before I placed my faith in Christ alone for salvation. But the moment I believed in Jesus, I was taken off the slave market of sin so that I am now free to obey the Lord and not be enslaved to sin. The Holy Spirit, Who lives inside me, can empower me to say "No" to sin and "Yes" to Christ. But if and when I do sin, the Holy Spirit will convict me so I can confess my sin to God and be restored to closeness with Him.

God made you and me, but He lost us through our sin, separating us from Him. But God came to earth and repurchased us by shedding His blood on the cross. We now belong to the Lord Jesus, and He is our Master. Let's thank Him by living for Him!

"I can't; God can. I think I will let Him."

The best decision of my life was the complete surrender and redemption of my life to Christ on 9/18/18. Baptism declares that you are a follower of Jesus Christ. It is a public confession of your faith in and commitment to Jesus Christ. It is the next step after salvation through repentance and faith and is an essential foundation for the Christian life.

Pastor Paul had me join him on his left side in the lake at the campground I wrote about earlier. I was wearing the long white sundress that my mother had bought me. I shared my testimony by giving my public confession of faith in front of my church congregation and my family.

Pastor Paul helped me cover my face as he lowered me under the lake water as a burial of my old life; coming up out of it was a resurrection. God raised me from the dead as He did Christ. I COULD NOT RESPOND TO God when I was stuck in my old sin-dead life.

God brought me alive – right along with Christ! Think of it! All sins are forgiven; the slate wiped clean. Pastor Paul brought me back to the surface, cleansed and pure of my sin.

I buried my "old life," and I rose to walk in a "new life."

Recently, our youth Pastor Brad was preaching at church. He said something that was a mic drop moment for me. So much so that I turned to his wife Kaylah and said, "O man, that was good." I heard a few "Amens" and viewed a few head nods at those words. It was the simplest non-complex way to move from sin and follow Christ.

"When you step out of sin, you step into HIM."

MIC DROP MOMENT!!!!!!!

There is someone who will never forsake you, no matter what you have done, no matter how dim your past, how awful you feel inside, how dreadful life treats you, how small you think you are. He will remain regardless. Our God is steadfast in everything. He loves us more than we ever know and feel. You must obey.

CHAPTER TWENTY-ONE
SERVANT HEART AND HANDS

Even when we are unfaithful, God is faithful. Despite our sins, He is still faithful. Gratitude for God is a powerful motivator. God doesn't want us to be motivated by dutifulness or guilt or just doing the right thing, but by gratitude for His incredible kindness and patience.

I am personally motivated to live as God has intended for me to do so. Developing a servant mentality was not especially hard for me. I attribute this to my mother. Growing up, she always had a servant's heart in everything she did.

I, to this day, get asked why I do so much for other people. I take this as an opportunity to tell my testimony, my story from sin to Christ. Explaining that when Jarred had passed away, I didn't want to do things the way I had done when Jacob passed away. I dropped to my knees and prayed to God for direction. I decided to become obedient when the Holy Spirit spoke to me, telling me what to do.

I quickly learned what having a servant's heart meant. I began to treat everything like a ministry. This dumbfounds people for some reason.

A servant's heart means we will give of ourselves even when we may feel like there is nothing to give to someone else. God can use us to accomplish many things in other people's lives if we learn to share our time, love, money, and words, and expect nothing in return.

Basically,

"To keep what we have, we must give it away."

We are called to be servants, are we not? Well, what does a servant do? He (or she) carries out the will of his master. A servant doesn't tell his master what to do -- they perform whatever tasks the master requests of them. A servant doesn't choose what days or times it's most convenient to serve their master. A servant's function is to follow and obey their master's instructions. A servant does not develop a vision for the master either. The master is the one with the vision -- and he wants his servants to be ready and available to carry out that vision and bring it to fruition.

How can we experience fulfillment in our lives? Simply by serving our Master - our Heavenly

Father. The world encourages us to seek counterfeit fulfillment – power, success, prosperity. The more of these things we gain, the more our flesh wants. It is our sinful human nature. We will never find true fulfillment when we seek these things.

We must become servants if we want to experience true fulfillment. We need to become modest, meek, and humble. As God's servants, we should have no other agenda except to do His will. When we become faithful to His will, He will fulfill the aspirations He desires for us in our lives… and even those we desire!

As God's faithful servant, I want to share in His success, have direct access to His power and wealth, and be able to walk in His authority! Once you get your heart in servant mode, you can watch how God brings about all we need and want.

Matthew 24:46

"Blessed is that servant, whom his Lord when He cometh shall find so doing."

You can start serving right now, where you're at. I can tell you without any reservation that when the Holy Spirit spoke to me after my son Jarred passed, it changed my circumstance. Being told to do good deeds and help as many people as possible was my new way of life. I was determined to serve, and one hundred percent committed to following God. Losing Jacob and Jarred were tragic events in my life. However, I can say without any reservation that my process of grieving and mourning with Jarred was a beautiful process.

Before you open your email to send me a snot gram about saying what I just did, let me explain. I am NOT saying that Jarred's death was beautiful; it was a terrible event, and it was agonizing. Nothing that I said or did could bring him back to life. God called him HOME to his eternity. I couldn't change the circumstances of his death, but I sure did change the perspective I had in my mind surrounding what took place.

I got a good spanking from above when Jarred died. God knew how bad things could get for me, from both losing Jacob and my life of Wicca. He knew this because He knows every hair on my head and every motive behind my actions. He watched every step I made in witchcraft, each spell I cast, and gave me the free will to do so.

The Holy Spirit gave me instructions, and I was obedient for the first time in my life, in every sense of the way. Developing a servant's heart was the catalyst for my healing. I started on day one and have continued without ever looking back.

God knew exactly what I needed, exactly when I needed it. He knew every flaw, thought, and immoral thing I had done. YET, I was chosen to serve others. In helping others, I healed myself in memory of my son Jarred.

Trust it, Trust His Ways and Trust His Name!

Proverbs 3:5-6

"Trust in the Lord with all your heart and lean not on your own understanding; in all your ways submit to Him and He will make your paths straight."

CHAPTER TWENTY-TWO
IN THE LIGHT OF ETERNITY

Being old and growing old is greatly valued. This is an expression of honor. At least when teaching and leading, there was a bias toward the people who are older.

Proverbs 16:31 says,

"Gray hair is a crown of glory. It's a sign of age and it's to be celebrated. And older people are to be honored."

Leviticus 19:32 says,

"You shall stand up before the gray head and honor the face of an old man."

It was the elders who led Israel. Disrespect for elders is an indication of societal breakdown. There is no retirement from the work of the kingdom. Until He calls us home, God wants to work in us and through us. We should use whatever capacity and gifts God gives us to serve Him. Don't fret about what you can't do, do what you can.

We allow "things" to get so wrapped up and upset that it dictates how we live here on this Earth. Even if we are Christians, this life's "temporal" things can quickly get our attention off Jesus. It will help if you can ask yourself, "In light of eternity, what does this "thing" matter?"

The vast majority of people pay no attention to eternity. They're living for the here and now, which is a waste because everything that's "here and now" isn't going to matter in five minutes, much less 50 years, and certainly not for eternity. If we stretched a rope from New York to Tokyo, that represents all of eternity, your life on Earth would be represented by less than one millimeter.

So how do you live in the light of eternity? You live for God's glory because He will share His glory with you in heaven.

You don't get to choose what will happen to you for the rest of your life. But you do get to decide how you respond. You can face the future as a cynic, as a critic, as a pessimist, or as a doubter. You can face the future, expecting the worst and experiencing the worst. You can face your future by being ungracious to other people, and you can live for the glory of yourself.

Or you can face the future with gratitude, generosity, and graciousness, and live for the glory of God. Which one do you think will make you happier? Which one do you think will make you more successful? Which one do you think will bring a smile to God and the reward of heaven?

We were created because God wants a family. He wants to spend eternity with His family. He wants to spend eternity with you and me! Heaven is one of the important reasons Christians can be joyful - God has given us eternal life, and heaven will be amazing!

I had a long conversation with a friend named Jacquie. I'm thankful she is always willing to help me process my thoughts before any speaking engagement. While I was preparing to officiate my nephew's memorial service, she said, "No one is getting out of here alive. This life is but an intermission of the big show. You better get your ticket; that price has been paid!" This is the true meaning of everlasting love. MIC DROP MOMENT:

"TEAR MY TICKET FOR ADMISSION."

Psalm 39 helps us put life in perspective by asking God to teach us that our lives are short and that meaning in life is found only in God. Let's walk through the Psalm.

Psalm 39 teaches us that we need to live our lives in the clear awareness and conviction that life is short, and apart from Christ-life is meaningless. It is the determination to focus on what matters because every day spent doing secondary things is spent not doing the most important things, like loving God and loving those around me. Sure, secondary tasks must be done, but those secondary (perhaps even good) things can consume my time and replace the primary things over time.

PSALMS 39

"I said, "I will watch my ways
and keep my tongue from sin;
I will put a muzzle on my mouth
while in the presence of the wicked.

So, I remained utterly silent,
not even saying anything good.
But my anguish increased;

Angela Rodgers

My heart grew hot within me.
While I meditated, the fire burned;
then I spoke with my tongue:

Show me, Lord, my life's end
and the number of my days;
let me know how fleeting my life is.

You have made my days a mere handbreadth;
the span of my years is as nothing before you.
Everyone is but a breath,
even those who seem secure.

Surely everyone goes around
like a mere phantom;
in vain they rush about, heaping up wealth
without knowing whose it will finally be.

But now, Lord, what do I look for?
My hope is in you.

Save me from all my transgressions
do not make me the scorn of fools.
I was silent; I would not open my mouth,
for you are the one who has done this.

From Darkness to Light

Remove your scourge from me;
I am overcome by the blow of your hand.

When you rebuke and discipline anyone
for their sin,
you consume their wealth like a moth -
surely everyone is but a breath.

Hear my prayer, Lord,
listen to my cry for help;
do not be deaf to my weeping.
I dwell with you as a foreigner,
a stranger, as all my ancestors were.

Look away from me, that I may enjoy life again
before I depart and am no more."

I am so thankful that I learned a better way. If I were still practicing witchcraft and not following God's word, my eternity would be one of hell and despair.

CHAPTER TWENTY-THREE
CONCLUSION: GOD'S PRETTY SMART

Through the pain of losing my sons, when I felt unworthy even to walk this earth because I felt that there was a chance that my past Wicca practices were the cause for what had taken place, I learned the right and the wrong way to do things.

Sadly, the wrong way was nothing less than complete self-destruction, and the written way led me to my new life of Christianity. For one thing, I am confident that God gave me grace when I did not deserve it.

I have been told I am an "intense person." I am never quite sure if that is meant kindly or complainingly, probably some of both. Either way, I thank God that the course of my life has allowed me to be intensely in love with Christianity.

After almost four years since being baptized, my love for God continues to grow daily, not through any strength of my own, but simply because my belief is infinitely deep and beautiful.

I am okay with being intense about something that I am passionate about.

God knew what He was doing when He spared me from death from my practice of Witchcraft. He spared me when I wanted to end my own life when Jacob died. He knew that I had a bigger purpose. He knew that I had a more significant role in our messed-up world today.

When we look at the path through which God is leading us and see the 'nails' that pierce our soul, do we sometimes wish it could be different? That life should be more comfortable, that the most challenging experiences are done away with? If we think like this, we suggest that God does not know what He is doing.

Everything that happens to a child of God (both the good and the bad) aids their divine purpose. But it's the uncomfortable, the challenging, and the painful that yield the best results as far as our spiritual growth is concerned. Not that God takes any pleasure in our pain, just that we simply do not grow in comfort as human beings.

Let's be honest, how many of us would still pursue God if we lived our ideal life? If we had all the material wealth we desired, with smooth-running relationships, good health, and everything went as expected, how many of us would keep God at the center of our lives? You do not have to be the most intelligent person to know that the most committed believers tend to be those who have had some challenges.

I am convinced that if we could fulfill our divine purpose without trials, God would never let a single one of us hurt, not even for a moment. Adversity was never in His original plan, and the only reason He exposes us to any is so that we can know His strength.

Adversity is undoubtedly not good, but good things can come from it.

Through the adversity of my life, God forgave my path to Him. He forgave that dark, dirty, twisted road that led me to Him.

I know that although I am redeemed and forgiven, I also know that I will still face a day of possible judgment one day for my sin and indiscretions. I know I hurt a lot of people in my journey.

The path of the narrow road that I take now is my path to eternity. Jesus compares the narrow gate to the "broad road," which leads to destruction (hell), and says that "many" will be on that road. By contrast, Jesus says "small is the gate and narrow the road that leads to life, and only a few find it."

IN THE LIGHT OF MY ETERNITY, THIS IS WHAT MATTERS.

Once I left witchcraft for my path with Christ, I used to stay up through the night still remembering the three-fold rule that Wicca had and thought "What if this is correct?" I had to spend a lot of time getting past what I did. In the beginning, I feared my judgment. I will have to answer for my actions one day, but Karma Christianity isn't Christianity at all.

There are plenty of cases where we might need to deal with the ramifications of our errors. Natural implications can make our lives more difficult because of our stupidity. But in the Bible, God wants us to know that He's not dealing with us according to karma. Instead, Romans 5:6 says,

"When we were still powerless, Christ died for the ungodly."

We didn't deserve any of it, but He did it anyway because He loves us.

Let this undeserved love permeate your life. When you have an exceedingly terrible week, you've messed up just about every project, you've treated your family horribly, most people in your life are upset with you, and you know it's all your fault, you will naturally think that God must be mad at you too. He may not be happy about how you've handled things, but when you believe in Jesus, that anger is averted. Honestly, when you're God's child, even when everyone else is mad at you, God's not mad at you. Because Christianity isn't about karma, it's about grace.

When you've been rejected by every boyfriend or girlfriend, every prospective employer, or your family, it is hard not to feel like a worthless waste of humanity. You might naturally think that if no one else wants to be around you, why would God? But when you are in Christ, God is delighted in you! He longs to be around you. He lights up when He sees your face, even if it seems like no one else does. Because Christianity isn't about karma, it's about grace.

It doesn't matter who you are, where you've been, how long you've rejected God, or how icky you feel when you think about your past. God wants you to know He doesn't deal with you on a performance basis. If He did, no one would make the cut. Instead, He comes to you when you're running away. He helps and encourages you. He blesses you and promises you perfect things.

Because that's just what He does, He's all about grace – love that you never deserved. But it's yours.

Isn't authentic Christianity so much better?!

CHAPTER TWENTY-FOUR
THE WHOLE ARMOR

After reading this one might begin thinking, "How do I protect myself from this evil?" Christians are fighting this as a daily battle. Not against flesh and blood, but against the powers of darkness. Believers do battle with fallen angels called demons, lead by Satan. These enemies of God and of ours attack believers on a consistent basis. What can Christians do to arm themselves against these spiritual attacks? How can a believer fight off these spiritual attacks? God has provided a way. It is found in the Word of God – the Bible – and it is there that we can "armor up."

We are told that we must put on the armor of God to be able to defend ourselves against the schemes of the Devil (Ephesians 6:9). In the bible Paul, having been under arrest so often by the Roman authorities, was familiar with the Roman Soldier's apparel. He thought it was the perfect analogy for the Christian in their fight against the invisible enemy of darkness. The Bible describes just what the armor of God is:

From Darkness to Light

Ephesians 6:10-17

¹⁰Finally, be strong in the Lord and in His mighty power.

¹¹Put on the full armor of God, so that you can take your stand against the devil's schemes.

¹²For our struggle is not against flesh and blood, but against the rulers, against the authorities, against the powers of this dark world and against the spiritual forces of evil in the heavenly realms.

¹³Therefore, put on the full armor of God, so that when the day of evil comes, you may be able to stand your ground, and after you have done everything, to stand.

¹⁴Stand firm then, with the belt of truth buckled around your waist, with the breastplate of righteousness in place,

¹⁵and with your feet fitted with the readiness that comes from the gospel of peace.

¹⁶In addition to all this, take up the shield of faith, with which you can extinguish all the flaming arrows of the evil one.

¹⁷Take the helmet of salvation and the sword of the Spirit, which is the word of God.

Satan does not concern himself with the world. He is not interested in them because they are already headed down the broad path of destruction. Those who do not believe in Christ do not need persuasion to sin. They are already held captive by the god of this world (II Corinthians 4:4). He also may not waste much time attacking so called carnal Christians. Those believers who live in a way that is not growing in grace, in holiness, and in the knowledge of God are no threat to the Devil. No, those who Satan sees as his arch enemies are those who are trying to live a holy life. He particularly hates those who are sharing the gospel of Jesus Christ. Even though he has already been defeated, he focuses his energy and sends his demons against those who are actively proclaiming Jesus Christ as the one and only way to heaven.

Spiritual attacks seem to most frequently occur at times of personal growth in the believer, when a Christian is overcoming a major sin or addiction, and when they are sharing their faith in Jesus Christ with others. We give far too much credit to the Devil. Remember that he was a created being and can never be God's equal.

I believe that spiritual attacks may be on the increase. Christians feel that the way this world is going we may be living in the last days before Jesus Christ returns. Although no one knows the day nor the hour of His return, we can clearly see the signs (Matthew 24). Satan must also realize that his time is running out before Jesus Christ returns to bind him and toss him into the Lake of Fire (Revelations 20:10).

CHAPTER TWENTY-FIVE
INVENTORY YOUR ARMOR OF GOD

How do you put on the armor of God? It really isn't as difficult as you think. All of the pieces of your armor are found in your relationship with Jesus.

Do you sometimes feel weak? Do you find yourself giving in to temptation when you really want to overcome? Are you ever discouraged? We all face these moments. But clothed in the whole armor of God, the weakest of His children is more than a match for Satan.

Still confused? Let's take a look at each piece of this spiritual armor and see how it can enable you to be victorious as soldiers for Christ in your battle against the "spiritual hosts of wickedness."

The Belt of Truth

Truth is the belt that holds the believers' armor together as well. Ultimate Truth can be found in God's Word. We must know this Truth in order to protect ourselves against our flesh, the world, and the Father of Lies. Truth grounds us and reminds us of our identity in Christ. Scripture should influence the way we live, raise our kids, do business, vote, and engage our communities. We are trying to rescue those who have been ensnared by false teaching, theological or otherwise.

The Breastplate of Righteousness

As believers, we have no righteousness apart from that which has been given us by Christ. Our breastplate is His righteousness. His righteousness will never fail. Though we have no righteousness of our own, we must still, by His power, choose to do right. Living a right life, rooted in God's Word, is powerful in protecting our heart, killing our flesh, and defeating the enemy.

Shoes of the Gospel

We don't give much thought to footwear, but the Roman army's shoes allowed them to travel further and faster than their enemies. The Roman soldier's footwear is what enabled him to travel on his journey. Likewise, the shoes of the gospel are what equips us to travel over rough roads as we carry this same gospel to others. As soldiers of Christ, we must put on "gospel shoes" that will allow us to march wherever our Lord leads.

The Shield of Faith

Faith is the shield of the believer. Trusting in God's power and protection is imperative in remaining steadfast. When the battle rages, we must remember that God works all things for good. He is always true to His promises.

The Helmet of Salvation

Be intentional about feeding your mind with spiritual food throughout the day. Load up your podcast with sermons from the greatest preachers in the world. Play those podcasts every single day on the way to and from work.

Sword of the Spirit

Our sword is the Word of God, both the written and the incarnate Word. Every other piece of armor protects us against attacks. With God's Word, we are truly able to fight and defeat all enemies. Christ used Scripture to defeat Satan when He was tempted in the desert. We must do the same.

Prayer

Before you do anything else, go straight into prayer. I start every day asking God for the wisdom to make good decisions, the discipline to stay true to His word, and the vision to hear His voice for direction.

CHAPTER TWENTY-SIX
THE TRUTH BEHIND THE CRAFT
THE GOOD, BAD AND UGLY

The facts of Witchcraft are very different than the actual impressions. Regardless of what the media, movies, and Hollywood portray, it isn't all glamour and lights. It is darkness like no other.

Some might think that these last few chapters should have been integrated into the book according to the events on my path. I considered that but had to decide if I wanted the gruesome truths of some of the things I experienced to overshadow my path to Christianity.

Although it is part of my path, I wanted to give the option for you to forgo reading this part because, 1) It's nearly impossible to understand that this kind of thing takes place, and 2) It is much easier not to know it happens so you can continue to look the other way. Regardless, you have a choice to read it or not.

Some, after reading this, will call me a Conspiracy Theorist. I'm okay with that. At least I am an educated one, because I know the world this chapter will be about. Everything I stated previously is the absolute truth regarding my path through Wicca, and how I found Christianity, I just cushioned the specifics to make it appropriate for most to read. What follows are the parts that are missing from my story.

Most follow the path to witchcraft for its power and significance. Little do they know, or understand, Satanism is all about SELF; you do what you want to make yourself feel good. Many Wicca rituals do not follow Satanic or Luciferian rituals, but there are just as many that do. Many things that I saw did resemble Satanism, and at times, even Luciferian. One thing I know without any reservation is that the Bible explicitly states multiple times the expectations on this. Scripture strongly advises against following idols other than God. Idolatry, in this sense, means abandoning the way of God for another aim. The Bible says we should put living in a righteous manner above all other pursuits of the flesh and mind. This takes me back to the Wide path and Narrow road.

Therefore, I believe Satanism, Luciferian, and Witchcraft are so popular today because people don't like rules and want to follow their own whims and desires. It's not a decision about black or white magic because it's all the same; it is Evil and is a one-way ticket to hell. Interestingly enough, Satanists and people who practice witchcraft dislike Christians because they feel they have to have a "book" (The Bible) tell them what to do. But oddly enough, they follow a self-made book of a different kind.

I was taught that Christianity was a joke; Satanism goes for the pillars. It possesses you and makes you someone you don't even recognize. Looking back at some of my rituals, I am still in absolute awe at God's grace He gave me. I surely didn't deserve it.

To be clear, I never practiced some of what you are about to read, but I do know that it does exist. But in full transparency I sadly did engage in a lot of it. I got out in time, and I thank God for that every day of my life.

Satanists are disciples of EVIL; following Satanism is not following our Savior. You can NOT be a Christian and be a witch simultaneously. The name Wicca literally translates to the word Witch. It is Witchcraft.

There are tons of Biblical proof that there is a Satan. Society has evidence of this as well. You cannot deny the existence of Satan without denying what scripture says. That's a lot to balance. Especially in the society that we currently live in.

TRIGGER WARNING AND DISTURBING CONTENT WARNING AHEAD

THE FOLLOWING CHAPTERS INCLUDE ALARMING CONTENT. I ENCOURAGE EVERYONE TO PREPARE THEMSELVES EMOTIONALLY BEFORE PROCEEDING. I DID NOT WANT THIS CHAPTER IN THE MAIN BOOK BECAUSE I WANTED TO OFFER A CHOICE IN IT BEING READ.

SOME OF THE TOPICS COVERED ARE HUMAN SACRIFICE, ANIMAL SACRIFICE, BLOOD RITUALS, SEX RITUALS, SATANIC AND LUCIFERIAN TOPICS.

IF YOU BELIEVE THAT READING THIS WILL BE TRAUMATIZING, YOU MAY CHOOSE TO FORGO IT AND SKIP AHEAD TO CHAPTER TWENTY-NINE. I WROTE THE BOOK SO THAT MY STORY WOULD STILL BE TOLD BEFORE THIS. BUT I ALSO KNOW AND UNDERSTAND THAT THERE ARE SOME WHO WILL WANT MORE. THIS IS MY TESTIMONY AND JOURNEY; SOME OF THE THINGS YOU ARE ABOUT TO READ WILL BOTHER YOU.

CHAPTER TWENTY-SEVEN
WHAT AM I ABOUT TO WRITE?

Let's dig into a bit of the "holiday" and "ritual," but before I do, be warned that your jaw may fall off your face as it hits the floor. Because some of what you are about to read will seem so farfetched. You're going to call my mother and tell her I need to be admitted into the stress unit. I promise you, 1) she already knows, and 2) that writing this is of no benefit to myself. It is uneasy for me to do given the topics.

But I believe that if we keep our mouths shut about what is truly happening in our world, we are not helping anyone.

If you are not worried about the world we live in after reading the following, I don't think you are human. Again, these are events and rituals that I know personally have taken place; I am not saying that I did partake in each one, but I have participated in some of them to be transparent.

Again, God's grace every day, AMEN. Most of these are directly related to Satanism and Luciferian practices, but many of them do cross over into Wicca. Either way you choose to look at it, not one of these is God-like or the pathway into Heaven.

Jan. 7 ~ ST. WINEBALD DAY (Blood Ritual)

Animal and/or human sacrifice and dismemberment.

Jan. 17 ~ SATANIC REVELS (Sexual Ritual)

Oral, anal, and vaginal, female age 7-17.

Jan. 20 – Feb. 2 ~ GRAND CLIMAX (Sexual and Blood Rituals)

Abduction, ceremonial preparation & holding of sacrificial victim for Candlemas. Oral, anal, vaginal, and human sacrifice.

Feb. 2 ~ CANDLEMAS (Sabbat Festival, Satanic Revels) (Sexual and Blood Rituals)

Oral, anal, and vaginal, human and/or animal sacrifice.

Feb. 14 ~ Valentine's Day (*HUMAN SACRIFICE*)

Feb. 25 ~ ST. VALPURGIS DAY (Blood Ritual)

Communion of blood and dismemberment.

Mar. 1 ~ ST. EICHATADT (Blood Ritual)

Drinking of human blood for strength and homage to Satan.

Mar. 20th or 21 ~ SPRING EQUINOX (Sabbat Festival, Major Fertility Sabbath dates vary) (Orgy Ritual))

Oral, anal, and vaginal; human and/or animal sacrifice.

GOOD FRIDAY through Easter Sunday (Death of Christ, dates vary) (Blood Ritual) (*HUMAN SACRIFICE)*

"Good Friday" is the beginning of satanic high days celebrated throughout the weekend to the end of the day on Easter Sunday. Pray with us for the rescue of all people being held for human sacrifice at this time.

EASTER EVE DAY (date varies annually) (Blood Ritual) *(HUMAN SACRIFICE)*

April 19 is the first day of the 13-day Satanic ritual day relating to fire, the fire god, Baal, or Moloch/Nimrod (the Sun God), also known as the Roman god, Saturn (Satan-Devil). This day is a significant human sacrifice day, demanding a (Fire sacrifice) with an emphasis on children.

Apr. 21 ~ GRAND CLIMAX (thru Apr 30) (Sexual and Blood Ritual)

Abduction, ceremonial preparation & holding of sacrificial victim for Walpurgisnacht Oral, anal, vaginal, and human sacrifice.

Apr. 30 ~ WALPURGISNACHT (Blood Ritual)

Animal and/or human sacrifice.

May 1 ~ BELTANE (Fire Festival, Coven initiations) (Fire and Orgy Ritual)

HUMAN or Animal SACRIFICE (this day happens to be my birthday, so there was significance there).

Jun. 21 ~ SUMMER SOLSTICE (date varies annually) (Sex and Blood Ritual)

Oral, anal, vaginal, and human and/or animal sacrifice.

Jul. 1 ~ DEMON REVELS (Blood Sacrifice)

Druids' sexual association with demons Age: Any age (female).

Jul. 20 ~ GRAND CLIMAX (thru Jul. 27, date varies annually, its five weeks, one day after Summer Solstice) (Sexual and Blood Ritual)

Abduction, ceremonial preparation & holding of sacrificial victim for Lammas Day Oral, anal, vaginal, and human sacrifice.

Aug. 1 ~ LAMMAS DAY (Blood Ritual)

Animal and/or human sacrifice.

Aug. 3 ~ SATANIC REVELS (Sexual Ritual)

Ritual Abuse: Oral, anal, and vaginal.

Sep. 7 ~ MARRIAGE TO THE BEAST SATAN (Orgy and Blood Ritual)

All females (especially children) in the cult are married to Satan in full bridal wear. Oral, anal, and vaginal, animal and/or human sacrifice, dismemberment.

Sep. 20 ~ HARVEST, MIDNIGHT HOST (Blood Ritual)

Dismemberment, hands removed of the victim for the "Hands of Glory" to Satan.

Sep. 23 ~ FALL EQUINOX (Orgy Ritual)

Oral, anal, and vaginal; human and/or animal sacrifice.

Oct. 13 ~ Continuous High Holiday (reverse date of October 31st)

Oct. 28 ~ SATANIC HIGH HOLY DAYS thru Nov 4. (Blood Ritual)

Abduction, ceremonial preparation & holding of sacrificial victim for All Hallows Eve Human Sacrifice.

Oct. 31 ~ ALL HALLOWS EVE (Halloween or Samhain) (Sex and Blood Ritual)

Sexual association with demons called up, and animal and human sacrifice.

Nov. 4 ~ SATANIC REVELS (Sexual Ritual)

Ritual Abuse: Oral, anal, and vaginal.

Dec. 21 or 22 ~ WINTER SOLSTICE (Sabbat Festival) (Sexual Ritual)

Oral, anal, and vaginal; human and/or animal sacrifice.

Dec. 24 ~ DEMON REVELS (High Grand Climax) (Orgy and Blood Ritual)

Sexual association with demons called up, and animal and/or human sacrifice.

Note: **Human sacrifices occur from Christmas Eve through New Year's Day.**

As if this wasn't terrible enough to read, I will say, "Hold my beer, even though I don't drink." Here are a couple of highlights of all the insanity you just read.

- The highest ritual holiday is the member's birthday. It usually involves the member or a victim of the member's choice and someone in authority, the coven's leader.
- The first and third of every month. Put 1 and 3 together, and it makes 13, though ritual/worship can occur at any time,

frequently coinciding with times of stress.

- All Friday the 13ths are high satanic days.
- All full-moon nights provide a reason for significant occult activity (most accessible to move around without difficulty and without being detected).
- Holy week (Palm Sunday to Easter Sunday). Some groups are thought to sacrifice, cook, and eat a human baby on Easter Sunday. (Yes, re-read this, it happens).

Satanic Ritual Abuse (SRA) is the real "secret" that keeps the Satan-worshiping demons in worldly power.

This is a subject that Christians want God's comfort but don't want the truth told because they're afraid to rock the boat... **but my God can walk on water, and I am a great swimmer.**

Thankfully, there are some brave Souls and Real Heroes who have investigated SRA and brought the reality of this hidden evil into the light.

The Blood Cult goes back many millenniums and is still ruling through banking bloodlines and masonry. The sacrifices are unthinkable to a human being with a Soul, and especially those of us who belong to Christ.

Those unfamiliar with this topic need to be aware that it is shocking and unthinkable for those with a conscience.

Yet, to turn away from the truth of the entire Satanic organized crime network is to enable it to continue. My heart would not allow that.

If we love Christ, we love the truth... no matter where it leads us.

Human trafficking and Pedophilia are connected to Satanic Ritual Abuse.

An abomination that is too terrible to mention or speak of, yet too much evidence has been presented to refute its existence.

Pedophilia, child abduction, Moloch worship...

Satanic ritual abuse. This is the evil that mature Christ-followers must look at and not bury their head about its existence.

Ezekiel 9:4

"And the Lord said unto him, Go through the midst of the city, through the midst of Jerusalem, and set a mark upon the foreheads of the men that sigh and that cry for all the abominations that be done in the midst thereof."

CHAPTER TWENTY-EIGHT
WHAT THE HELL DID I JUST READ?

If you're currently saying this to yourself, I'm glad. Mission accomplished. I bet some of you are still shaking your head and going, "no way."

It is estimated that at least 8 million children worldwide go missing each year. It is estimated that nearly 800,000 children will be reported missing each year in the USA; 40,000 children go missing each year in Brazil; 50,500 in Canada; 39,000 in France; 100,000 in Germany; and 45,000 in Mexico. An estimated 230,000 children go missing in the United Kingdom each year, or one child every 5 minutes.

Ask yourself these questions:

Who is benefiting from the enslavement of human beings on earth?

Who is benefiting by having sex with our children?

This is a massive epidemic today.

Human trafficking involves the use of force, fraud,

or coercion to obtain some type of labor or commercial sex act. Every year, millions of men, women, and children are trafficked worldwide – including right here in the United States. It can happen in any community, and victims can be any age, race, gender, or nationality.

Traffickers might use violence, manipulation, or false promises of well-paying jobs or romantic relationships to lure victims into trafficking situations. Traffickers use force, fraud, or coercion to lure their victims and force them into labor or commercial sexual exploitation.

They look for people who are susceptible for a variety of reasons, including psychological or emotional vulnerability, economic hardship, lack of a social safety net, natural disasters, or political instability. The trauma caused by the traffickers can be so great that many may not identify themselves as victims or ask for help, even in highly public settings.

There are many forms of Human Trafficking: Debt Bondage, Sexual Slavery, Organ, Forced Labor, and Child Soldiers are generally the forms of Human Trafficking we hear about.

But none of us look to the underlying issue with the potential Luciferianism and Satanism rituals.

Bottom line:

THIS IS HUMAN TRAFFICKING JUST AT A DIFFERENT LEVEL.

Many individuals can be involved in this, including recruiters, the Elite, document providers, transporters, CORRUPT OFFICIALS, and employers. But what we are not hearing much about is the correlation between Cults and their level of involvement.

Let me poke the bear for a moment. Are you still skeptical? I get it; I do.

And if you're asking yourself, HOW DO THESE PEOPLE GET AWAY WITH THIS? Have you not yet figured out that the very people who are supposed to end it might be the ones doing it?

Matthew 18:6-6

"If anyone causes one of these little ones- those who believe in me to stumble, it would be better for them to have a large millstone hung around their neck and to be drowned in the depths of the sea."

It is all written; there is a manual that has been around for thousands of years. It's a one-book, tell-all way to live read. It's the only way. We currently live in a scary society, and what is happening to our children should frighten all of you. But guess what, as parents, you're the only ones who can educate them on the dangers and give them a foundation to ward off these attacks, because they are everywhere...

I hope that you were able to take a few things away from reading my Darkness to Light story. I appreciate you more than you know and the Grace you gave me while reading.

I know I touched on some tough topics here, I'm only one person, and this is just my story. There are so many others out there that are afraid to stand up and be bold about theirs. The time to be BOLD is now.

God revives communities by first changing lives in those communities. As individuals go from death to life, lost to found, bound to free, sick to healed, demonized to delivered, there is then tangible evidence of the love and power of God at work. These stories spread hope in families, neighborhoods, towns, and cities.

This is how spiritual awakenings begin. Testimonies tear down demonic strongholds and reveal just how real and personal Jesus is. Our diversity enables us to reach more people. So, don't be ashamed of your story. Could you share it? Walk out your faith in front of others. Talk about what

Jesus has done in your life. This can be done at any moment of any day.

Mark 9:42

"What did Jesus say, God will have the last word on this."

CHAPTER TWENTY-NINE
A GLITCH IN REALITY

When will people open their eyes and connect the dots? When will people stop calling me a conspiracy theorist and actually ask some honest questions? Even some of the very people that are fighting child trafficking and human trafficking don't want to connect the dots. Some of these same people are the ones who are begging for funding from politicians or Elite's directly responsible for these disgusting acts worldwide.

Personally, I am extremely blessed with the team I work with to rescue and protect the vulnerable. I trust my team and we have each other's "6". I also know that not everyone has that same blessing. I have heard so many horror stories of influential people actually taking part in, covering up and benefiting from this "reality glitch."

The reality is this has been going on for thousands of years by some very influential people and those whom they control. The circle of elite businessman and even SOME Ecclesiastical Governments and SOME Free Masons around the world have been doing this in style as society claps them on. They pretend to bust a few pedophiles locally and claim they are fighting the war on child trafficking when it's just another publicity stunt to calm the masses. The reality is however, behind the scenes, children are taken from places all around the world. I've seen it firsthand in my travels and in my own hometown.

It enrages me when I'm called a conspiracy theorist by people so cowardly, they wouldn't dare do a single thing in defense of children or people in their life. As they sit in an office pretending that they're "normal" working hard for the man. They watch a few Netflix shows and pretend they are experts on child trafficking with their feminist rhetoric hating on men.

The reality is in satanic ritual abuse (SRA) and child trafficking it is common to have a mother or female family member line up their abuse. I've personally seen this happen…. Multiple times.

This isn't always the case, there are the cases like you see on TV, a man meets a girl, befriends her, becomes her boyfriend, then the abuse and trafficking begin. This does happen all the time as well and is equally disgusting.

The hierarchy of the Ecclesiastical Government, Jesuits, and even some Free Masons makes it all too easy to hide the satanic games they play. Secret passages, tunnels, and secret cities aiding them along the way. Using presidents as mere puppets as they hook them up on an island of boys for their pedophilic dreams. Who dare speak out when they will reveal your past to the public as you get slaughtered in jail. No one bats an eye when another whistleblower commits "suicide." How dumb do you have to be to continue believing the news and their propaganda as they normalize, sexualize, and protect pedophiles and their sex with children?

I'm not talking just about your uncle Billy who molested a few children in your family, but rather an entire system created and devoted to satanic ritual abuse of children worldwide.

Many fighting child trafficking claim it's for money. Are you really that stupid? Why would a billionaire, trillionaire, or head of state risk his entire reputation and freedom for a few dollars to traffic a child? No, you silly puppet, it's far more sinister and satanic whether you want to believe in Jesus Christ, Satan, or God is literally irrelevant. THEY DO worship Lucifer. THEY DO sacrifice children for reasons you will never understand unless you seek out the truth for yourself. Using these children for their blood or sexual gratification is only a piece of the puzzle as they chant for devils and demons in the backwoods. It's very real and you shrugging it off is exactly what they want.

Just another crazy person talking badly about the global elite, right? Except what do I have to gain? Where's my power and wealth for speaking out? I live like a hermit trying to expose the truth as I'm ridiculed and attacked every step of the way.

This is the reality I've lived for so long as I continue trying to raise awareness of the reality we dance on. These people pretend to "fight" trafficking like it's a game but behind the veil it's a full on spiritual war. It's time to wake up.

CHAPTER THIRTY
HOW TO MAKE HEAVEN YOUR HOME

This is probably one of the most important chapters in this book. I even saved it for last because I wanted you to close the book with it. After reading the heavy in the previous pages I want to end on a positive note. One that is one of the most important decisions you will ever make in your life.

"In the Light of your eternity, this is what matters."

Many people believe that the answer to the question of how to get to heaven is to be a good person. For some, being good means simply not being bad like:

- Not murdering anyone
- Not stealing
- Not cursing
- Not lying
- Not doing drugs
- Not cheating

Your conscience is clear because you aren't nearly as bad as the people you read about in the media. You're just like everyone else you know, and you can't all be going to hell. So, you're pretty sure that after you die God is going to let you into His heaven, right? Pretty sure?????

Many others believe that the answer to the question in how to make heaven your home revolves around doing good deeds like:

- Giving money to beggars on street corners.
- Giving food to the homeless.
- Being actively involved in your community.
- Generously donating your time and/or your money to non-profit and charitable organizations.

You're better than most of the people you know. In fact, you're so good that you're convinced that, after you die, God will absolutely let you into His heaven, right? Your Convinced???

There are others who believe that their religious rituals will be their ticket into heaven. The truth is that there is only one way for any human being to get to heaven and that is to believe in the Lord Jesus Christ.

Every human being is, by nature, a sinful being. The Bible says that our efforts at doing "good deeds" are not acceptable in the sight of God (Ephesians 2:8-9). God alone is holy. God alone is good. So, God has made a way for sinful human beings to enter into His heaven. I know that the good deeds I do won't earn my ticket to heaven, my obedience to God will.

Jesus died so that those who believe in Him would no longer be condemned to an eternity apart from God. If you want to be assured of going to heaven after you die, and you believe that Jesus Christ died to save you from the penalty for your sins, answer these questions:

Do you understand that you are a sinner, and you believe that Jesus Christ came as the one and only Redeemer of sin?

Are you ready to receive God's gift of His Son, Jesus Christ?

If so, believe in Christ, repent of your sins, and commit the rest of your life to Him as Lord.

The most important relationship for every one of us is our relationship with Jesus Christ. Choosing to believe that he is who he claimed to be - the Son of God and the only way to salvation - and receiving him by faith as your Lord and Savior is the most vital act anyone will ever do. We want life. He is Life. We need cleansing. He is the Living

From Darkness to Light

Water.

Are you ready to receive God's gift of His Son, Jesus Christ? If so, believe in Christ, repent of your sins, and commit the rest of your life to Him as Lord. Hit your knees and pray the following:

> **Jesus, I believe you are the Son of God, that you died on the cross to rescue me from sin and death and to restore me to the Father. I choose now to turn from my sins, my self-centeredness, and every part of my life that does not please you. I choose you. I give myself to you. I receive your forgiveness and ask you to take your rightful place in my life as my Savior and Lord.**
>
> **Come reign in my heart, fill me with your love and your life, and help me to become a person who is truly loving - a person like you. Restore me, Jesus. Live in me. Love through me.**
>
> **Thank you, God. In Jesus' name I pray. Amen.**

If you decided to receive Jesus today, welcome to God's family, send me an email and let me know.

Now, as a way to grow closer to Him, the Bible tells us to follow up on our commitment.

- Get baptized as commanded by Christ.
- Tell someone else about your new faith in Christ.
- Spend time with God each day. It does not have to be a long period of time. Just develop the daily habit of praying to Him and reading His Word. Ask God to increase your faith and your understanding of the Bible.
- Seek fellowship with other followers of Jesus. Develop a group of believing friends to answer your questions and support you.
- Find a local church where you can worship God.

The End, but it is just my beginning.

What's Next
(Working Titles)

365 Daily Devotional for Grieving Parents

After the Death Of a Child
Co-written with Troy Steven

Our Adoption Stories

Parenting In The World We Live In Today

From Darkness to Light

CONNECT WITH ME?

www.Angelamrodgers.com

For speaking engagements, please email:
Contact@Angelamrodgers.com
FB: @AuthorAngelaRodgers

For Human Trafficking education contact
Millstone Ministries
FB @MillstoneMinistry18.6

If you would like your book personalized, please send personalization instructions along with a pre-Paid self-addressed return envelope to:

Author Angela Rodgers

PO box 544

Owosso, MI 48867

If you enjoyed this book and think it will help others, please take a few moments to write a review on your favorite store, and refer it to your friends.

Made in the USA
Columbia, SC
05 June 2022